BLISSFIELD

An American Mystery

Douglas Post

BROADWAY PLAY PUBLISHING INC
New York
www.broadwayplaypublishing.com
info@broadwayplaypublishing.com

BLISSFIELD

© Copyright 2003 by Douglas Post

Cover art: Jason Lee

First printing: June 2016
I S B N: 978-0-88145-668-4

Book design: Marie Donovan
Word processing: Microsoft Word
Typographic controls: Xerox Ventura Publisher 2.0 P E
Typeface: Palatino
Printed and bound in the U S A

BLISSFIELD was first produced at the Victory Gardens Theater (Dennis Zacek, Artistic Director) in Chicago, Illinois, on September 15, 2000. The cast was as follows:

CARTER BARTOSEK..Kevin Gudahl
BEN OGLESBY ....Patrick Bresnyan
SALLY OGLESBY..Jane Blass
BETH MCALISTER HARPER ....Kelly Hazen
ZOE HARPER ....Bethany O'Grady
REVEREND ROY MCALISTER............................Tom Roland
ERNIE NOODLEMAN ....Jeff Still
DEXTER DEFILLIPIS....................................Patrick Thornton
LOIS GARRITY.. Mary Ann Thebus

Director ....Dennis Zacek
Set design ....Jack Magaw
Costume design ....Judith Lundberg
Lighting design ....Todd Hensley
Sound design .... Andre Pluess & Ben Sussman
Production stage manager ....Tina M Jach

CHARACTERS & SETTING

CARTER BARTOSEK, *a foreign correspondent*
BEN OGLESBY, *a real estate attorney*
SALLY OGLESBY, *a registered nurse*
BETH MCALISTER HARPER, *a church secretary*
ZOE HARPER, BETH's *daughter*
REVEREND ROY MCALISTER, *a minister*
ERNIE NOODLEMAN, *a manager of a riverboat casino*
DEXTER DEFILLIPIS, *a police commander*
LOIS GARRITY, *a retired teacher*

All are in their late 30s and early 40s except for ROY *and* LOIS *who are in their 60s and* ZOE *who is seven.*

Time: Spring
Place: The town of Blissfield, IL

This play is dedicated to
Dennis Zacek,
Marcelle McVay,
and the founding members of
the Victory Gardens Playwrights Ensemble

"No matter:
the country of our childhood survives,
if only in our minds,
and retains our loyalty
when casting us into exile;
we carry its image from city to city
as our most essential baggage."
Malcolm Cowley

"O lost, and by the wind grieved, ghost, come back
again."
Thomas Wolfe

ACT ONE

Scene 1

(The attic of Dan Harper's house in the Midwestern town of Blissfield, Illinois. Spring. Monday morning. CARTER BARTOSEK, *early 40s and fatigued, is crouched in the corner of the room with his hand covering his mouth. He wears soiled work clothes, which he appears to have been sleeping in for a week. A weather-beaten bag lies on the floor next to him.* BEN OGLESBY, *the same age and dressed in a black suit, stands apprehensively inside the doorway. He stares at* CARTER *who is staring at a large wooden desk with a simple chair. Behind the chair is a wall, which has been cracked apart by three bullet holes. Two of them are to the side of the chair and several feet above it. The third is directly behind it. The area around this last hole is covered with a solid smattering of dried blood.* CARTER *removes his hand from his mouth. He takes a deep breath and speaks.)*

CARTER: Did you say something?

BEN: I asked if you were okay.

CARTER: I'm okay.

BEN: Because you looked like you were about to be sick.

CARTER: Yeah, I thought I was, but I'm…I'm alright, really I…God, this is harder than I expected.

BEN: I know.

CARTER: I mean, I see dried blood seven times a day, so I should be able to handle it, right?

BEN: Do you want to go?

CARTER: No. *(He stands up.)* Shouldn't there be tape? Police tape? Wrapped all around this house?

BEN: They took it down over the weekend.

CARTER: That was fast.

BEN: Yeah, well, it didn't take long to make a determination.

CARTER: Suicide.

BEN: Right.

CARTER: I can't believe it.

BEN: No, me neither, but you can't argue with the facts.

CARTER: Which are?

BEN: Oh, come on, Carter.

BEN: I want to know.

BEN: Okay. *(Pause)* He was turning forty-three and he wanted a huge blow out. A bacchanal. A few hours into it we could see he was unsteady. Stumbling into things. I helped him into the house. We all went home. Around midnight the cops came by and— *(Pause)* There was a gun on the floor. A semi-automatic. The back of his skull… *(Pause)* Well, he'd evidently fired off a few shots at his temple that missed their mark. Then he managed to aim the thing at the center of his forehead. He was lying there. Blood everywhere. It was…

CARTER: A mess.

BEN: Yeah. *(Pause)* Anyway, they had to do an autopsy even though it was fairly obvious what had happened. He'd been drinking a lot that night. Well, we all had.

CARTER: How drunk would he have to be to miss his own head?

BEN: There was something else running through his system. Some pain killers. Perca…perco…something.

CARTER: Percocet?

BEN: It's a narcotic, right?

CARTER: Oh, yeah. Highly addictive. A colleague of mine was hooked on them.

BEN: Well, that's not all. The desk drawer had evidently fallen out when he reached for the gun. The contents were scattered all over the floor.

CARTER: More pills?

BEN: Worse.

CARTER: Money?

(BEN *shakes his head.*)

CARTER: Body parts?

BEN: Pornography. Little girls. He'd been collecting pictures of little girls.

CARTER: Jesus Christ.

BEN: I know, I know, it's not the Dan Harper we'd grown up with, but he'd been away, okay? He'd changed. And this, I guess, was the end result.

CARTER: What was he doing back here?

BEN: You didn't know?

CARTER: Ben, I haven't talked to Danny in six years.

BEN: He was running for mayor.

CARTER: You're kidding me.

BEN: No. He'd left D C. He said he was disgusted with that life, the amount of money it took to mount a campaign, the time, the energy, and nothing left to do what he set out to do in the first place.

CARTER: Yeah, well, after four consecutive terms in that lovely community, I'm surprised he could even remember.

BEN: He came home last fall after his mom died to settle the will and sell the house. And he couldn't leave. He said he couldn't go back. He loved this place. He wanted to make a difference.

CARTER: To be mayor?

BEN: Hey, old man Westheimer's retiring and he was more than happy to throw his weight behind the golden boy. Dan glided through the primaries. The generals were two weeks away.

CARTER: And he was a sure thing.

BEN: Oh, yeah, everybody loved him.

CARTER: Except, apparently, the man himself.

BEN: Hard to believe, huh?

CARTER: Impossible. *(He goes to a window and looks out.)* I mean, I look out this window and I'm seventeen again. We all are. Running down Eldridge Road through Dooley's Woods to this house out here in the middle of nowhere. This attic. It was like my refuge from the world.

BEN: Yeah, for me, too.

CARTER: I had my first beer up here.

BEN: I had my first cigarette.

CARTER: Yeah, I remember that. You puked all over the rug.

BEN: No, I didn't.

CARTER: You turned twelve shades of purple. Me and Dan were worried to death. Thought we'd disrupted your delicate sensibility.

BEN: I was never delicate.

CARTER: No, but you were sensible.

BEN: You were reckless.

CARTER: Was not.

BEN: You brought those girls up here from Floral Park when Dan's folks were out of town.

CARTER: Well, nothing happened. We all emerged virgins. I thought we could impress them with the plans the three of us had to change the map of the world.

BEN: These days I'm lucky to change a real estate ordinance.

(CARTER *laughs.*)

CARTER: Still running the law firm?

BEN: When it's not running me.

CARTER: Yeah, well, we all had our aspirations.

BEN: What are you saying? Aren't you doing what you always wanted to do? Circling the hemisphere?

CARTER: I don't do a lot of circling, Ben. Mostly I sit in one place and talk to people. I'll tell you, I get so burnt out on the suffering. The plain stupidity and meanness and misery of it all. For what? For turf mostly. Twenty feet of sand that's mine and not yours. So boom. Goodbye. God approves. (*He shakes his head.*) I think about this place a lot.

BEN: Really?

CARTER: Oh, yeah.

BEN: Why?

(CARTER laughs.)

CARTER: Well, I guess it wouldn't mean as much to you. Living here all your life. It's like breathing. Or good health. You take it for granted.

BEN: What?

CARTER: The fact that there's one spot on earth where chaos doesn't rule. Where people are still concerned about something other than their own few crumbs of the cake. I carry that with me. I don't mind telling you. It means something.

(Pause)

BEN: So how did you find out?

CARTER: About Dan?

(BEN's cellular phone rings.)

BEN: Excuse me. *(He answers it.)* Hello? Yeah. Yeah, I'm at Dan's. With Carter. No, he called me. I met him at O'Hare. I don't know, I'll ask. *(To CARTER)* Do you want to go to the funeral?

CARTER: Of course.

(BEN finishes the call.)

BEN: Yes. Where are you? Because in two minutes you could be here. Because we need to get him some clothes and I've got to go on ahead. Yes. Yes, alright. *(He hangs up.)* That was Sally.

CARTER: How's she holding up?

BEN: Not well.

CARTER: She still with the hospital?

BEN: And the Junior League. And the Jubilee Book Fair. And whatever else she's thrown herself into this week. I swear, it's like she's afraid to stand still. Like she'll dissolve if there's a single non-productive moment in her day.

CARTER: So life is full.

BEN: Too full. *(Pause)* So you were telling me—

CARTER: I was in Beirut. Filing a story. I saw it on C N N. "Former Congressman Found Dead In Midwestern Home." I took a cab to the airport and caught the first flight out. I didn't even pack a bag.

BEN: I would have called, but—

(BEN's phone rings again.)

BEN: Pardon me. *(He answers it.)* Hello? No, the front door's unlocked. Okay. Okay. *(He hangs up.)* We're in a constant state of communication.

CARTER: I can see that.

BEN: She's nervous about seeing you.

CARTER: Why?

BEN: I don't know, Carter. We've been married almost twenty years and I still don't understand the way her mind works. Tell her she looks good, okay?

CARTER: Okay.

(SALLY calls up from downstairs.)

SALLY: Hello?

BEN: We're up here.

(A moment. Then SALLY OGLESBY appears in the doorway. She is the same age as BEN, wears a black dress, and is somewhat erratic.)

SALLY: I don't want to come in.

CARTER: I don't blame you.

(CARTER goes to SALLY and gives her a full embrace.)

CARTER: Hello, Sal.

SALLY: I can't believe you're here.

CARTER: You look great.

SALLY: Oh, God, I look so wretched I could cry.

CARTER: Not to me.

SALLY: How'd you get into the house?

BEN: One of the cops was on his way out. He—

CARTER: It was my idea. I wanted to see where it happened. To try to make sense of it.

SALLY: Well, good luck.

CARTER: Right.

SALLY: Because it's so illogical it makes my brain rattle. And try explaining to a teenage son and his eleven-year-old brother that their godfather who they worshipped more than their own dad— *(To BEN)* I'm sorry, honey, they love you, they do, but it's a strange age, for both of them— *(Back to CARTER)* Benji has an eating disorder and Joey wears a dress with a diamond tiara—

BEN: Around the house.

SALLY: Yes, only around the house, but try explaining to those two that the man who once took them biking and hiking and horseback riding was actually a pervert with a taste for pills.

BEN: You didn't tell them that.

SALLY: No, of course, I didn't tell them that, but I had to say something. And they can see it on the news. They know what people are saying.

BEN: Are they with your folks?

SALLY: Yes. I really didn't think that the service would be appropriate for them. Maybe it is, but I don't know.

BEN: They should be there.

SALLY: Fine. Go and get them. I'll get Carter a suit.

CARTER: I don't want to be any trouble.

SALLY: You're not. But you can't go looking like that. Not that you don't look wonderful. It's wonderful to see you. *(She embraces him again.)* It's just all so awfully, awfully sad.

(SALLY starts to cry, pulls herself away, and goes back downstairs. A moment. BEN and CARTER look at each other.)

BEN: Ready?

CARTER: Sure. *(He goes to his bag. He pulls out a camera and focuses it. Then he takes a picture of the attic.)*

BEN: What are you doing?

CARTER: Oh, I don't know. Force of habit, I guess. I take photos of everything these days.

BEN: Well, don't turn the camera on me, alright?

CARTER: Alright.

BEN: I'm supposed to speak at this thing. Say something. I feel all busted up inside.

CARTER: Me, too. *(Pause)* Where's the ceremony?

BEN: The church. The First Presbyterian. Roy McAlister's officiating.

CARTER: So she'll be there?

BEN: Who? *(Pause)* Oh. Yeah. I mean, I would assume.

CARTER: Okay. *(Pause)* Let's go.

(BEN and CARTER walk out of the room.)

Scene 2

(The office of the REVEREND ROY MCALISTER at the First Presbyterian Church. Monday afternoon. The sound of organ music is heard outside the room, which holds a desk with a chair and a second chair facing it. The light from a

large stained glass window hits the floor. It catches BETH
MCALISTER HARPER, *who is a few years younger than*
CARTER, BEN *and* SALLY. *She is slender, attractive and
dressed in dark colors.* BETH *is kneeling down before her
daughter,* ZOE, *an advanced seven-year-old.)*

BETH: Please listen.

ZOE: I am.

BETH: This is important.

ZOE: Okay.

BETH: Because you're going to hear a lot of different
things. A lot of different people are going to want to
talk to you. To say how sorry they are. But what's
important, what really matters about all of this, is…
Honey, look at me.

ZOE: What?

BETH: It was an accident. A horrible accident. I don't
believe that your father would ever do anything to
intentionally hurt himself. And he certainly wouldn't
want to see you hurt. By any of this.

ZOE: Can we go home now?

BETH: No.

ZOE: Why not?

BETH: Because there are people out there who want to
share their sorrow.

ZOE: Like Melanie Lester?

BETH: What?

ZOE: If Melanie Lester's out there I don't want to go.

BETH: Why?

ZOE: I just don't.

BETH: Did she say something to you about your dad?

ZOE: She's always saying *something*.

BETH: You know that he loved you. In his way. He tried to be there for you.

ZOE: I know that, Mom. I'm not totally ignorant. But—

BETH: It still hurts.

ZOE: That's not it.

BETH: Then what?

(ZOE *shakes her head.*)

BETH: Tell me.

ZOE: I just don't think he should have come back here.

BETH: No.

ZOE: Especially if he was going to go away.

(Pause)

BETH: Oh, sweetheart— *(She reaches out to* ZOE.*)* Come here.

(ZOE *goes into* BETH's *arms and* BETH *wraps herself around her daughter.*)

BETH: My little angel. I love you. So much.

(ROY, *an energetic man in his sixties who likes to be at the center of things, walks into the room.*)

ROY: Well, it's worse than I thought.

BETH: How so?

ROY: The attendance. It's miserably low. There's a scattered assortment of twenty or thirty people on the main floor and a few professional mourners in the balcony.

BETH: I'm surprised.

ROY: Why?

BETH: Well, the way people around here worshipped him, the sense that he could do no wrong, I would have thought there'd be an outpouring.

ROY: Yes, well, it's pouring the other way.

ZOE: Grandpa, are we still going to the new mall on Saturday?

ROY: Of course, we're going to go. Of course, we are. Why wouldn't we?

ZOE: I don't know, I thought, maybe… *(She shrugs.)* Things change.

ROY: That's right. Things change. They do. Sometimes for the better. And sometimes not. Sometimes fate is as fickle as the wind. We can't see the plan. But we have to trust that there's a meaning. For everything. And my feelings for you are rock solid. Steady as this church. I am always going to be here for you.

ZOE: Always?

ROY: Always. In one way or another. I will be right…

(ROY grabs ZOE and tickles her. She laughs.)

ROY: Here.

ZOE: Stop!

(ROY gives ZOE a kiss. She smiles at him. Then she turns to BETH.)

ZOE: Mom, can I draw?

BETH: Of course, you can, honey.

(ZOE climbs up into ROY's chair, empties the contents of her bag out onto his desk, and finds a pencil. He attempts to pull BETH to one side. He speaks in a lower tone.)

ROY: How are you doing today?

BETH: I'm okay.

ROY: Are you eating?

BETH: Some. She had a huge meal. Pancakes and sausages.

ROY: Look, Beth, I know that things were bad at the end—

BETH: Not now, Dad.

ROY: That you and Dan had your difficulties, especially through the divorce, and before—

BETH: Not now.

ROY: But if you feel the need to talk, to air your feelings—

BETH: There's nothing that I need to talk about and I know how I feel.

ROY: Okay, alright, but you might want to take a few days off.

BETH: And do what?

ROY: Well, I—

BETH: Aren't you addressing the Chamber of Commerce on Thursday?

ROY: Yes.

BETH: And then there's the Bradfords' wedding over the weekend?

ROY: Yes, but—

BETH: So there's work to do. We have a church to run. Unless you don't want me here.

ROY: Of course, I want you here.

BETH: Then please, please let me worry about how this affects me. And her. *He* made a decision. I don't understand it. But I have a life here, which has to go forward.

ROY: Yes, I understand that, but—

(BEN *enters.*)

ROY: Hello, Ben.

BEN: Reverend. Beth, how are you?

BETH: Better.

BEN: I'm sorry I'm late. I got cornered by these media people on the front steps. Everyone wants to know the real story.

BETH: What did you say?

BEN: What could I say? I can't say anything. I don't know anything.

ROY: Media?

BEN: Yes, there're cameras and reporters all over the parking lot.

BETH: That might explain it.

BEN: What?

BETH: Why people are staying away.

ROY: No one wants to be affiliated with a failure.

BEN: It's worse than that.

ROY: Yes, of course, it's worse than that. It's unforgivable. Well, almost. We have to forgive. And forget. But I've been with this congregation for twenty-seven years now—

BETH: Twenty-eight.

ROY: Yes, and I've never seen anything like it.

BEN: Is Sally here?

ROY: I don't think so.

BEN: She was bringing Carter.

(BETH *looks up.*)

ROY: Carter Bartosek?

BEN: He found out and flew in. I invited him to the service. To meet with us beforehand.

ROY: Of course. That was absolutely the right thing to do. I know how close you boys were. Did you hear that, Beth? Carter's coming.

BETH: Yes, I heard, I— *(Pause)* I have to get some water.

(BETH walks out of the room. A moment. ROY turns to BEN.)

ROY: Not a good day.

BEN: No.

(Silence. ZOE draws in a book. BEN and ROY shuffle their feet.)

ROY: How are you, Ben?

BEN: Fine.

(More silence)

ROY: Has there been any…new information?

BEN: I've been with my family all weekend. I haven't had a chance to talk to anyone else.

ROY: No, of course not. *(Pause)* Well, I did mention, I had the opportunity to make a phone call last night. Actually two. Two calls. First Rupert Frost. Then Paul Ehrenhart. And they both said, regarding the loan, that it's only a matter of—

BEN: I'd rather be talking about something else.

ROY: Of course.

(Pause)

BEN: I don't know what to say today. At the service. About Dan.

ROY: May I make a suggestion?

BEN: Alright.

ROY: Speak about the man he was. The one everyone admired. Before this.

BEN: Pretend it never happened.

ROY: In a sense, yes.

(SALLY *enters with* CARTER, *who is now wearing a dark suit.*)

SALLY: Is this the right day?

ROY: Yes.

SALLY: Because there's no one out there.

ROY: We'll be out there. We'll make it a ceremony to remember. Carter, is that you?

CARTER: Reverend McAlister, it's good to see you again.

ROY: Good to see you, too, son. Good to see you, too.

(*They shake hands.*)

CARTER: I almost didn't recognize the place.

ROY: What, the church?

CARTER: The new sanctuary.

ROY: Yes, completely renovated. And refurbished. Got a new pipe organ, memorial windows, teak pews—

CARTER: The Founder's Tower looks like it's been restored.

ROY: Brick by brick. Still the tallest building in the area. With a bell we had cast in the Netherlands.

CARTER: Really?

ROY: Carter, you should hear that baby ring.

CARTER: I can't believe Central Avenue. It's all so—

ROY: Cleaned up?

CARTER: Yeah.

ROY: Well, after the last plant closed, we had to do something. The town was economically devastated. Things were falling apart. The church was the cornerstone. After that, we rebuilt the bridge. Then the Arcadia Hotel and the Buffalo Cinema. Resurfaced the facades. Spruced up the storefronts. Revived the entire downtown.

CARTER: Well, it's astonishing.

ROY: Tell him, Ben.

BEN: We, uh, won the Great American Main Street Award.

CARTER: Really?

ROY: And truly.

CARTER: I'm impressed.

ROY: So, Carter, are you here alone? Is there a wife? Children?

CARTER: No, I…never married.

ROY: That's right. I remember. So what are you doing now? Wait. Don't tell me. Military service? Something overseas?

CARTER: I'm still a reporter. A foreign correspondent. For a small paper.

ROY: God, that's wonderful! And here you are today. When it seems like two seconds ago, all of you were boys, girls, slamming books together, singing in the choir, running track.

CARTER: Yeah.

ROY: I still remember that meet. The mile relay race in Champaign. First place in the state.

CARTER: That was a day.

ROY: You and Ben and Dan. You made me so proud. Made this town proud.

SALLY: Hey, I was there, too.

ROY: Of course, you were, Sally. Remind me now.
Were you…athletic?

SALLY: No, but I rallied pep.

ROY: That's right.

SALLY: Raised school spirit.

ROY: I remember.

SALLY: Well, in those microscopic skirts they made us
wear we raised more than spirit.

BEN: Sally—

SALLY: What?

BEN: There's a child present.

(CARTER *sees* ZOE *on the floor.*)

CARTER: Who's this?

ROY: Zoe, my granddaughter.

CARTER: Of course.

(*A moment. Then* CARTER *walks over to* ZOE *and kneels
down beside her. She ignores him.*)

CARTER: God, she's as pretty as her mother.

ROY: You've never met?

CARTER: No. Well, we'd all…fallen out of…

(BETH *comes back into the room. She stands at a distance,
watching* CARTER. ZOE *looks up at him.*)

CARTER: Hello, Zoe. I'm Carter. I was a friend of your
dad's. And your mom's. We all…we grew up together.

ZOE: I'll be seven in two weeks.

CARTER: Really?

ZOE: Shannon Kent isn't coming to my birthday party.

CARTER: Oh, why is that?

ZOE: Because she wrecked my paint set and called me a stuck-up pig.

BETH: Hello, Carter.

(CARTER *turns and sees* BETH. *He stands. A moment*)

CARTER: Beth.

BETH: It was nice of you to come. To be here. It would have made him…happy.

CARTER: Well, I wouldn't be anywhere else.

ROY: Remarkable. How long has it been? Since you two have seen each other?

CARTER: Uh— (*He looks at* BETH.)

BETH: When were you here last?

CARTER: Almost ten years ago. My folks retired to Michigan. I helped them with the move.

BETH: Then that was it. Ten years. We would have seen each other then.

(CARTER *nods.*)

CARTER: Right.

ROY: Well…

(*Silence*)

BETH: Don't we have a special prayer for the occasion, Dad?

ROY: Of course, we do.

BETH: Zoe?

ZOE: What?

BETH: Put your pencils down.

ROY: Let's form a circle, shall we? Hold hands? Have a moment of silence?

(*They all come into a circle and close their eyes.*)

ROY: Jesus said, "Come to me, all who labor and are heavily burdened, and I will give you rest." Let us pray for our brother, Daniel, that he may rest from his labors, and enter into God's eternal light. Receive, O Lord, your servant, for he returns to you.

Scene 3

(BEN *and* SALLY's *backyard. Monday evening.* BEN, CARTER, *and* BETH *are standing around an assortment of lawn furniture. They are still dressed in their clothes from the funeral.* BEN *and* CARTER *are drinking beers while* BETH *sips a soda.*)

BEN: Alright, we can say it. It's no secret. Public speaking has never been my strength.

CARTER: I don't think you should dwell on it.

BETH: Definitely not.

CARTER: It was fine.

BETH: It was more than fine. Honestly, Ben. It was moving.

CARTER: It was. Incredibly moving. More so than if you'd actually said…words.

BEN: Did I say anything at all?

CARTER: Well, there were sounds. The formation of language. I think everyone in the church knew what you were feeling.

BETH: I'm sure of it.

BEN: I went absolutely blank.

CARTER: It happens.

BEN: Totally lost.

BETH: It gave the rest of us time to reflect.

BEN: I got up there. I pulled out my notes. And I had nothing to say for…how long?

CARTER: Not that long.

BETH: No.

CARTER: A minute.

BETH: Maybe two.

CARTER: Two. Tops.

BEN: Christ, I knew I should have had some breakfast.

(SALLY *comes toward them.*)

SALLY: The caterers are standing around staring at their feet.

BEN: Let them eat something.

SALLY: I did. I told them to help themselves. I can't believe we ordered this much food.

BETH: It's a beautiful repast, Sally, regardless of who came.

SALLY: What the hell are we going to do with two baked hams, all that herring, the hollandaise sauce—?

BETH: How are the kids?

SALLY: Oh, they're fine. They're upstairs. Zoe's sorting through Joey's dress collection.

BEN: Jesus, on top of everything else, my son, the cross-dresser.

SALLY: It's a phase, Ben.

BEN: Do we need more beer? We need more beer. I'll go. (*He walks off.*)

SALLY: My God, that was so embarrassing.

BETH: No, really, it wasn't.

SALLY: He stood there for five minutes and said nothing.

CARTER: It wasn't that long.

SALLY: It seemed that long.

CARTER: Hey, if it were me, I would have done the same thing.

BETH: So would I.

CARTER: Because finally, ultimately, what is there to say?

SALLY: What do you mean?

CARTER: The man took his own life. That's all we know. So better no speeches, no pontificating on the merits of his past, which are evident, or should be, to everybody in this community. I'm serious. I like the fact that Ben said nothing. There's not a goddamn thing to say. Except why. *(Pause)* I'm sorry, I'm a little fatigued.

SALLY: How long have you been on your feet?

CARTER: A while. A few days. I feel like I'm spinning.

BETH: Maybe you should sit down.

CARTER: I'm okay. *(He takes in his surroundings.)* Well, the new house is spectacular.

SALLY: It's larger than we need. Much larger. I keep running into rooms I forget are there.

CARTER: Did it come with the swimming pool?

SALLY: No. We had that put in. With the hot tub no one uses.

CARTER: Who owns the tennis courts next door?

SALLY: They're both ours. Ben wanted a second lot. Now we have two mortgages and no time to do anything but talk about debt.

(Pause)

CARTER: Well, the boys are beautiful, Sally. I can't believe how big they are. Last time I saw them Ben

Junior was raising hell in a three-wheeler and the little guy was spitting up formula.

SALLY: Well, we do it all for them. At least that's what I tell myself.

(SALLY *hears an argument in progress from the front of the house and looks off.*)

SALLY: Excuse me.

(SALLY *walks away. Silence.* CARTER *and* BETH *look at each other.*)

CARTER: So you're okay?

BETH: Yes.

CARTER: Really?

BETH: Really.

CARTER: Because it's an awful thing.

BETH: It is. Truly awful. I don't pretend to comprehend it. Can't begin to fathom it. But the man, well…he'd become a stranger to me.

CARTER: Things never got better, huh?

BETH: No. I went from being his trophy wife to an extension of his staff to someone he completely ignored. I'd barely spoken to him since he came back to town. I was surprised that he even invited me to his party. But I went. For Zoe.

CARTER: You've been living here since the divorce?

BETH: It'll be five years in September. Dad needed a secretary and I needed the steady income. He's a little lost since Mom died.

CARTER: I can see that.

BETH: So it's worked out.

CARTER: Your daughter…she's breathtaking.

BETH: Thanks.

CARTER: A little princess.

BETH: Oh, believe me, she knows.

CARTER: How do you mean?

BETH: The other day I caught her talking to her Barbie doll.

CARTER: What did she say?

BETH: "Do you think that I was put here on this earth to be your slave?"

(BETH *and* CARTER *both laugh.*)

CARTER: So you spoil her.

BETH: Yes.

CARTER: That's good. That's what children are for.

(Pause)

BETH: So where are you now?

CARTER: Me? Reporting from? Lebanon.

BETH: How long have you been there?

CARTER: Six, seven years. I cover the entire Middle East. But I base myself out of Beirut.

BETH: Beirut. My God. It seems like the other side of the world.

CARTER: Yeah, well, it *is* the other side of the world. *(Pause)* So I have to ask.

BETH: What?

CARTER: Manhattan. *(Pause)* Your dad didn't know.

BETH: No.

CARTER: Does anybody?

(Silence. BETH looks away. She doesn't respond.)

CARTER: Did Danny?

(But before BETH *can answer* DEXTER DEFILLIPIS *walks on followed by* ERNIE NOODLEMAN *and* SALLY. *The two men are the same age as* CARTER *and dressed in dark clothes from the service.* ERNIE *is the lighter personality of the two, although at the moment he is carrying a parking ticket and is clearly perturbed.* DEXTER *is darker, moodier.)*

ERNIE: So who are you trying to impress?

DEXTER: I'm not trying to impress anyone. I'm carrying out my commission. Pure and simple.

SALLY: Fellas—

ERNIE: Hey, Dexter, you're off-duty.

DEXTER: That doesn't mean you can thumb your nose at a city ordinance.

ERNIE: A parking ticket? For pulling up in front of a fire hydrant? Are you nuts?

SALLY: Listen, I really don't think—

*(*DEXTER *turns on* ERNIE.*)*

DEXTER: Here's the way it works, Noodleman. Ben Oglesby's out here charging up the grill. He gets a little enthusiastic with the lighter fluid. Suddenly the house catches on fire, the flame carries, and all these beautiful new homes go up in smoke. And the water boys are hanging onto their hose like a limp dingus. Why? Because a local entrepreneur with no sense of self-control thought he was better than the law.

*(*ERNIE *stares at* DEXTER. *Then he tears up the parking ticket and lets the pieces drop all over the ground.* DEXTER *looks at the fragments. He looks at* ERNIE. *Silence)*

Now you're littering.

SALLY: Let me take care of this.

*(*SALLY *hurriedly picks up the pieces of the ticket as* DEXTER *shakes his finger at* ERNIE.*)*

DEXTER: I'll deal with you later.

(DEXTER *goes to* CARTER *and extends his hand.*)

CARTER: Dexter Defillipis?

DEXTER: Hey, Bartosek, I thought I saw you at the ceremony.

CARTER: You're a cop?

DEXTER: What's so strange about that?

CARTER: Well, I have this dim recollection of you hitting a science teacher, running your Harley through a shop window, and, uh—

DEXTER: What?

CARTER: Setting a house on fire.

(DEXTER *shrugs.*)

DEXTER: I found some other hobbies.

SALLY: Dexter recently made Commander.

DEXTER: One of three. It's no big deal. I do what I always do.

ERNIE: Yeah, follow the municipal code like it came down from the mountain.

(CARTER *approaches* ERNIE.)

CARTER: And Ernie Noodleman.

ERNIE: Is there anything to eat?

CARTER: I'm relieved to see you finally made your way out of that locker the kids used to throw you in.

ERNIE: Childhood pranks. Meaningless episodes. Now I do the same thing to my customers.

SALLY: Ernie manages the Riverboat Casino in town.

CARTER: I saw the ship.

DEXTER: Like a painted whore in church.

ERNIE: So what do you do?

SALLY: Carter works overseas.

ERNIE: Oh. Interesting. How's the money?

CARTER: The money? *(He laughs.)* Oh, I'm rolling in it. Got a cattle ranch in Utah. And a chateau in the south of nowhere.

ERNIE: Hey, I've been there.

DEXTER: Haven't we all?

ERNIE: And I don't intend to go back.

*(*BEN *walks on carrying a cooler and a plate of food.)*

BEN: Okay, who needs something to drink? Oh, I forgot. I do.

ERNIE: And me.

DEXTER: Yeah, what the hell.

BEN: Beth, another soda?

BETH: No, it's getting late. We should go. Zoe has school tomorrow.

DEXTER: I'm sorry about your loss, Beth. Your daughter's loss.

BETH: Thanks.

ERNIE: Goes for me, too.

BETH: Carter, how long are you here?

CARTER: I don't know yet. I'm due back on Thursday. Maybe then.

BETH: You're more than welcome to stay with me. We have a house by the nature preserve. And an extra bed.

CARTER: Oh.

SALLY: I told him he could stay here.

BEN: There's plenty of room.

SALLY: He can have his own floor.

BETH: But with the boys—

CARTER: No, I'm okay. I think I'll camp out with Ben. Thanks, Beth.

BETH: Okay. *(Pause)* We should talk before you go.

CARTER: Right.

(Pause)

BETH: Well, goodnight.

(They all bid their farewells as BETH walks off and BEN serves a round of drinks. ERNIE takes the plate of food. He feeds himself and forgets to pass it around.)

ERNIE: Well, that was some service. Small in attendance, perhaps. But I felt like the people who wanted to be there really wanted to be there.

DEXTER: Yeah, that's true.

ERNIE: It was a fine affair.

CARTER: Yes, it was.

ERNIE: Except for that period of ten minutes when nobody said anything.

SALLY: Hey, guys, he already feels bad enough. Can we drop it? Please?

ERNIE: Sure. *(He lifts his beer.)* To Danny. Wherever he is. For whatever reason.

(They touch bottles and drink. A moment. No one says anything. CARTER pulls his camera out of his bag. He runs his fingers over it.)

CARTER: Anybody mind if I—?

BEN: No.

SALLY: No, go ahead, just don't take a picture of—

(CARTER takes a picture of her.)

SALLY: Me.

CARTER: Sorry, Sal.

(CARTER *then takes a shot of* BEN, *then* ERNIE, *then* DEXTER.)

ERNIE: For the memories, huh?

CARTER: Yeah.

ERNIE: Hey, I understand. I wish I had one of Danny Harper. Before he went blotto that night.

CARTER: You were there?

ERNIE: We were *all* there.

BEN: Ernie stayed with me after I sent Sally and the kids home.

ERNIE: Dan was obviously in no shape to do anything. He was weaving around. Talking funny. Ben took care of him. And I took care of the help.

CARTER: So you were the last people to see him alive.

ERNIE: Well, I'd have monitored his condition, but I promised the wife I'd put the twins to bed. And I had to be at the riverboat. Bright-eyed and bushy-tailed. I'll tell you, Carter, it's boom boom time down there. People can't throw their cash at us fast enough.

CARTER: Congratulations.

ERNIE: Yeah, man, I am shoveling it in.

CARTER: I meant the twins.

ERNIE: Oh. Okay. Thanks. *(Pause)* Can I get another beer?

(BEN *hands* ERNIE *one.*)

CARTER: So, Dexter, you must know the cops who found him.

DEXTER: I *was* the cop who found him.

BEN: Didn't I mention that?

CARTER: Uh, no.

DEXTER: I have to tell you that picture'll stick in my head till I'm old and bloated. All that wet blood. All that…waste.

BEN: He was the one who called it in.

DEXTER: Our people were out there in minutes. Of course, we haven't dealt with anything like this in recent memory, but they did good work. I mostly watched and tried to keep my stomach together.

CARTER: And then you had to go home to *your* wife and kids.

DEXTER: I live alone.

CARTER: Oh. *(Pause)* So, why?

DEXTER: Why what?

CARTER: Why did he do it?

(DEXTER *laughs.)*

DEXTER: Who knows why anybody does anything?

CARTER: No, I mean, here he is, finally out of the D C cesspool, free to pursue smaller political ambitions in his hometown, right, Ben?

BEN: That's what he said.

CARTER: He's on the cusp. The position is his. If he wants it.

DEXTER: Oh, he wanted it, alright.

CARTER: Okay, so two weeks before he takes over city hall, he throws a huge party at which he gets thoroughly trashed, goes into his house, and puts a gun to his head.

ERNIE: Don't forget the porn.

CARTER: I'm not forgetting it, Ernie. But, honestly, think about it. What sort of sense does any of this make?

ERNIE: My guess?

CARTER: Okay.

ERNIE: He wasn't happy.

DEXTER: Yeah, well, that's unbelievably brilliant.

ERNIE: It's the truth.

DEXTER: Hey, Ernie, who's happy? Ben?

BEN: Yes?

DEXTER: Are you happy?

BEN: Pardon me, Dexter, I don't mean to be insulting, but do you know any middle-aged real estate lawyers who are happy?

DEXTER: My point. Sally?

SALLY: What?

DEXTER: Happiness?

SALLY: Oh, I don't know. The kids make me smile. With their band rehearsals. And soccer practice. And the work I do at the hospital. The seniors seem to really need me. And the interns. And then there's the volunteerism. Raising money for teenage moms. Reading to kids in homeless shelters. Not in this area, of course, but I don't mind the travel. It keeps me busy. Keeps me active. *(Pause)* I can't say I'm always happy.

DEXTER: Okay, Bartosek, are you happy doing whatever it is you do?

CARTER: I don't know that I'd use that word.

DEXTER: Hey, if you have to flip through a thesaurus, forget it.

(Pause)

ERNIE: Well, I'm happy.

DEXTER: That's because you don't know any better.

ERNIE: Oh, nice. Real nice.

DEXTER: So there it is. Maybe we were all happy once. When we were high school sweethearts. Or cheerleaders. Or track stars. We were born and raised in one of the most beautiful locales in the Midwest.

CARTER: In the country.

DEXTER: Right. In the country. Life is apple picking and pot luck suppers. What's not to be happy about? Some of us appreciated it. Some didn't. We committed random acts of arson. Or got into a tussle with the wrestling team and found our underpants hung up in a tree while we were still wearing them.

ERNIE: Hey, that only happened once.

CARTER: We had a lot to be thankful for.

DEXTER: We did. That's a fact. Did we use it to our advantage? Did we blow it? *(He shrugs.)* Each man or woman has to speak for themselves.

CARTER: Do you remember what Lois Garrity used to say?

DEXTER: Not really. She got me thrown out of school. Twice.

ERNIE: Hey, I almost flunked her English class. I reminded her of that fact. At Dan's party.

CARTER: She was there?

ERNIE: She parked herself next to the booze table and held court.

BEN: She's retired now.

SALLY: But she still has an opinion or two.

ERNIE: Oh, yeah.

CARTER: I should check in with her.

DEXTER: So what did she say?

CARTER: About what?

DEXTER: Happiness.

(Pause)

CARTER: I can't remember. *(He stands.)* I think the jet lag finally hit me.

SALLY: Do you want to lie down?

CARTER: Please.

DEXTER: Nice seeing you again, Bartosek.

ERNIE: Yeah, come on by the boat and we'll go out for a spin. I got a couple of Mexican babes working the floor that'll make your nipples hard. Hey, Sally.

SALLY: What?

ERNIE: Is there any more food?

(SALLY stares at ERNIE and his empty plate.)

SALLY: No.

BEN: Goodnight, Carter.

CARTER: 'Night.

SALLY: Come to bed soon, okay?

BEN: Okay.

(CARTER and SALLY walk off. A moment. The three men sit in silence.)

BEN: Another beer?

DEXTER: No, I'm set.

ERNIE: No.

(Pause)

BEN: Can we talk about this?

DEXTER: No! We do not talk about this. Not now. Not ever. Thanks for the beer.

(DEXTER *stands and goes. A moment*)

BEN: Something went wrong.

ERNIE: Tell me about it.

(BEN *and* ERNIE *sit in silence.*)

ERNIE: Ben?

BEN: What?

ERNIE: *Tell* me about it.

BEN: I— *(Pause)* There's nothing to tell.

(*A moment. Then* ERNIE *laughs. He stands up.*)

ERNIE: Okay. Fine. *(Pause)* I'm going to go urinate in your tennis courts.

(ERNIE *wanders off in the opposite direction from* DEXTER *while* BEN *remains motionless on his lawn chair.*)

Scene 4

(LOIS GARRITY's *living room. Tuesday afternoon. Several stacks of old newspapers and magazines line the floor. A rumpled armchair rests to one side. In it,* LOIS, *late sixties, learned, and slightly drunk, reclines.*)

LOIS: How does a place become a place? Have you ever asked yourself this? Ever wondered? What was it that drew the first settlers to a specific location? Was it all a rush of happy accidents? A hurrying towards a particularly rude winter? Or was there foresight? Planning? How many times did they get it wrong before they got it right? Did they ever get it right? And what holds us here today? Why is this still our home? Have we all gone nuts? Gone native? Can we see no further than the edge of our driveway, the curve of our street, and so assume that the satellites got it wrong? That, in fact, the world is flat and we are living in the center of it?

(CARTER *enters from the kitchen, wearing clean clothes, and carrying a bottle of bourbon.*)

CARTER: This is, uh…the only…bottle I could find.

LOIS: There's a case of bourbon hiding somewhere in this house under all this clutter. Here. Let me dust that thing off.

(CARTER *hands* LOIS *the bottle, which she wipes against her house dress, opens, and pours into a glass at her side.*)

LOIS: I used to drink mint juleps and somehow managed to convince myself that I was covering the five basic food groups: mint, sugar, water, whiskey and ice. Then the cats ate all the mint in my garden. The store stopped selling bar sugar. My pipes burst. The freezer broke. And I was left with this. *(She drinks.)* My diet suffers, but I don't seem to care.

CARTER: Well, it's afternoon, Mrs G. And you're retired. I guess that you're allowed a cocktail.

LOIS: I started around seven.

CARTER: Oh.

LOIS: Tell me about yourself, Carter. I am so sick of my own noise that I can't bear it. Bombard me with information. Are you still based in Moscow? Or was it Beijing?

CARTER: China, then Russia. Now I cover the Middle East.

LOIS: Cairo?

CARTER: Beirut. It's the best place to be if you want to follow the flow of munitions. See what hell the U S is raising this week in the name of foreign aid.

LOIS: And who do you write for?

CARTER: Well, I freelance for two or three people, but most of my stuff ends up in this tiny, little publication called *The Expatriate*.

LOIS: I subscribe.

CARTER: Oh, so you're the one.

LOIS: Although, I haven't actually perused an issue in some time. My eyes are poor. And the print is small.

CARTER: Yeah, it keeps getting smaller and smaller, but somehow they manage to put it out.

LOIS: And do you ever get the urge to latch onto a larger outfit?

CARTER: What? Like *Useless News & World Distort*? Or a paper with colored pie charts and no story that goes onto page two?

LOIS: Have they offered you a post?

CARTER: Who?

LOIS: *U S News* or *U S A Today*?

CARTER: Well, no, but—

LOIS: So your moral stance has not been tested.

CARTER: It gets tested everyday, Mrs G.

LOIS: Yes, of course, it does. I only mean to suggest that you must want people to know what you do. You were always a great one for modesty, but, as I recall, it was mostly false.

CARTER: Really?

LOIS: Oh, yes. You're one of the most ambitious people I know. It's just that your proclivities have taken you on a rather circuitous route. Am I wrong? Is the whiskey ranting?

(CARTER *laughs.*)

CARTER: No, I suppose it's true. There are still a few people in this world whose respect I want. You're one of them.

LOIS: I have always respected you. Even when you turned in those horrendous reports that were such a rough approximation of the English language I had to howl. Even when your attempts at spelling were so bad they made my teeth hurt.

(CARTER *laughs again.*)

LOIS: Are you sad?

CARTER: What?

LOIS: About Daniel?

(Pause)

CARTER: I can't even begin to tell you.

LOIS: Try.

CARTER: Well, he...was like family to me. You know that. How close we all were. Me and Danny and Ben. The unholy three. Running. Why were we always running? I don't know. I could never keep up with him. He was always a little bit ahead of me. Leading me on.

LOIS: You were the better student.

CARTER: Yeah, but he had such ease with people. He never patronized. He just knew how to...connect.

LOIS: And you stayed in touch?

CARTER: All through college, our twenties, thirties, and then...I don't know. Dan and I took different paths. Different... (*Using her word*) Routes. The last time I talked to him... (*He shuffles around the room.*) It was difficult.

LOIS: Oh?

CARTER: I mean, the circumstances. His life was coming apart. He'd left Beth. He wanted his daughter. She didn't want him to have her. I…didn't know how to respond.

LOIS: And that was the last time you spoke?

(CARTER *nods. He moves through the room. A moment*)

CARTER: Had you talked to him at all since he came back to town?

LOIS: I had spoken with Daniel exactly twice. Once, at his party, last Friday night to say the briefest of hellos.

CARTER: Yeah, I heard you were there.

LOIS: Well, the booze was free, so I kept Ben company while he bartended.

CARTER: And the other time?

LOIS: When he was putting together his platform.

CARTER: I thought he was a sure thing.

LOIS: Oh, he was. The only other person running against him was a former school bus driver. But speaking to a congressional assembly and addressing a town of twenty-six thousand complacent Americans are two different matters. He saw things he wanted to do. And he needed to know how to go about them.

CARTER: Things.

LOIS: Yes.

CARTER: Such as?

(*A moment.* LOIS *looks at* CARTER. *Then she rises, shuffles over to a stack of newspapers, and starts sorting through the contents.*)

LOIS: What changes have you seen here since you've been back?

CARTER: Well, the downtown's taken off. It's almost bustling. There's all these new homes, new developments, like Ben's neighborhood. That's alright, I guess. But driving around this morning, I could hardly believe the landscape.

LOIS: The farm acreage?

CARTER: Gone.

LOIS: The forests?

CARTER: Leveled. And in their place all these office complexes. Industrial parks. Miles and miles of the ugliest terrain I have ever encountered. And that includes Tel Aviv.

LOIS: The Fortune Five Hundred people have discovered our little neck of the woods.

CARTER: Yeah, I recognized most of the names.

LOIS: We've gone from being an industrial community in decline to a high-tech hub.

CARTER: The town got richer.

LOIS: Oh, yes. Our property values have skyrocketed. You wouldn't believe what I've been offered for this miserable shack.

CARTER: What does this have to do with Dan?

LOIS: You tell me.

(CARTER *laughs*.)

CARTER: Okay, I'm fourteen again, and you're conducting the lesson.

LOIS: So far you would not get a passing grade.

(*A moment*)

CARTER: Dan Harper. Well, he was always looking out for the disenfranchised. The disinherited. He once told me there were two classes of wealth in this country.

Those who climbed the economic ladder and pulled it up after them. And those who reached back. He wanted to be reaching back. It's what got him into trouble in the Beltway.

LOIS: Correct.

CARTER: So?

(LOIS *turns on* CARTER, *exasperated.*)

LOIS: Damn it to hell, Carter, think! You saw the strip malls and shopping centers! Who parks those cars? Who tends those stores? Who cleans the sewers, the streets, the office complexes?

CARTER: No one who can afford to live here. *(Pause)* Is that it? Is that what he wanted to do? Make it so the working class outside this community had a way in?

(A moment. LOIS *looks at* CARTER. *Then she decides to continue.)*

LOIS: There's some condemned property near the center of town. Three blocks from the church and right on the river. Dan wanted to fill the space with an affordable housing development.

CARTER: Section Eight.

LOIS: Yes.

CARTER: Makes sense.

LOIS: Not to some.

CARTER: How do you mean?

LOIS: Well, he'd evidently run the idea by one or two people and gotten a bad response, so he came to me.

CARTER: And what did you say?

LOIS: I advised him to shut up about it. Our city council is essentially a social club. Once elected, he could do almost anything he desired.

CARTER: Did he follow your advice?

LOIS: Here. *(She finds what she has been looking for and drops a pile of newspapers at his feet.) The Standard Dispatch* dating back to the day Dan announced his run.

CARTER: God, they're still printing this thing?

LOIS: It's easier than not printing it. He's in there two or three times a week. There's not a word about affordable housing. Not a whisper about helping the less fortunate. Until— *(She throws a single issue at him.)* Three weeks ago. Page thirteen. Near the bottom.

(CARTER opens the paper and reads.)

CARTER: "Candidate Harper Denies Housing Plan."

LOIS: An unnamed source leaked Dan's idea to the newspaper. And he denied it. Said that it was too soon to contemplate such a move.

CARTER: Basically what you'd told him to do.

LOIS: Exactly.

CARTER: And the upshot?

(LOIS laughs.)

LOIS: Carter, this is Dan Harper we're talking about. The local hero. The crowned prince.

CARTER: Nobody cared.

LOIS: So two weeks ago the unnamed source tried the same thing with more details and more denials. *(She throws another issue at him.)* Page twenty-seven. Under the lingerie ad.

CARTER: They buried it.

LOIS: And last week they dropped the story altogether.

CARTER: Along with the unnamed source and this nasty little leak.

LOIS: Now you're thinking!

CARTER: What? *(Pause)* What am I thinking, Mrs G? *(Pause)* Who were these one or two people Dan talked to?

LOIS: About the development?

CARTER: Yes.

LOIS: He didn't say.

CARTER: But one of them obviously talked to the paper.

LOIS: Or someone they talked to.

CARTER: Did you speak with anyone?

LOIS: Of course not.

CARTER: So this person was frustrated in their efforts.

LOIS: I can only assume.

CARTER: And maybe they were so frustrated that they took the next step.

LOIS: Possibly.

CARTER: With a story certain to make the front page of this and every other periodical.

LOIS: Potentially.

(A moment. CARTER looks at LOIS. He laughs.)

CARTER: Okay, now, Mrs G, this is all starting to get a little sinister.

LOIS: Is it?

CARTER: A little nuts.

LOIS: Why's that?

CARTER: Well, you're saying that someone was so upset about this housing plan, so scared of its consequences, that they might have actually manufactured his—

(CARTER stops. LOIS stares at him. She doesn't say anything.)

CARTER: Demise.

LOIS: I'm not saying anything.

CARTER: Yeah, but the implication is that he was set up. To look like a suicide. Which is insane.

LOIS: You're right. It's insane. It makes much more sense that the Dan Harper we knew was a narcotics freak and a collector of smut. That he was starting his life over only to end it. So don't bother checking it out. Get on a plane. Go back to Lebanon. Where it's safe.

(CARTER *looks at the pile of newsprint at his feet. He looks at* LOIS. *He sighs.*)

CARTER: If I do this, if I go through the campaign material, the police reports, if I ask around, and I find that something's off-center—

LOIS: Yes?

CARTER: Then what?

LOIS: What did I teach you?

CARTER: Mrs G—

LOIS: What is the most essential rule?

(*A moment*)

CARTER: Tell the truth—

LOIS: And then?

CARTER: Run like hell.

Scene 5

(*The deck of the riverboat. Tuesday night.* DEXTER *sits on a bench running his fingers through a deck of cards while* CARTER *stands at the railing staring out at the water. We hear the sounds of disco music, dealers conversing, and*

*electronic slot machines inside the main cabin. The boat is
obviously crowded.)*

DEXTER: No, it is. I agree. Funny that we should all
share a passion for the same game. Because I probably
only said two words to Oglesby in high school and
even less to Noodleman. Then I happened to see
Ben here one night bottoming out at Blackjack and
Caribbean Stud. And I knew Ernie was a fan. So the
three of us formed a club.

CARTER: Texas Hold 'Em?

DEXTER: Hey, it's the Grand Prix of Poker and a good
waste of a Tuesday night. Afterwards Ernie docks the
boat and we drain a few beers at the Old Grist Mill.
Winner buys. *(Pause)* So you were telling me about
your busy day.

CARTER: Oh. Right. Well, I went to *The Dispatch* and
asked them what they had on this unnamed source
whose story got buried in the underwear ads.

DEXTER: And they said?

CARTER: They never talked to anyone. Never took any
calls. The information got dropped through their mail
slot. Early in the morning. In plain courier face.

DEXTER: Could be anyone. So what? What do you care?

CARTER: I think it's possible that Dan had an enemy.
Someone who knew his private agenda and wanted to
make it public. But also wanted to protect themselves
from the backlash.

DEXTER: Well, that I understand. You couldn't say
anything bad about the guy. It was like defacing the
flag.

CARTER: So I talked to his staff. His former staff. Such
as it is.

DEXTER: And what did they say?

CARTER: That he was concerned about the town. Its character. With all this new money. But they couldn't pin him down on specifics. And he never talked to them about this idea.

DEXTER: Maybe he was afraid they'd walk out the door.

CARTER: Meaning?

DEXTER: Affordable housing is a losing proposition.

CARTER: For who?

DEXTER: Hey, Bartosek, I don't know if you've noticed, but this community has been cleaned up considerably since you were here. The kids do not do drugs. The crime is minimal. People work. Shop. Sleep. That's pretty much it. And it's pretty much perfect.

CARTER: Okay.

DEXTER: Would you want to see us go the way of Grantham? Or Floral Park? Both towns are falling apart due to unemployment, property damage and gangs. The houses are in bad condition. The downtowns are blighted.

CARTER: Well, I haven't actually been to either place recently, but—

DEXTER: Believe me, don't go.

(Pause)

CARTER: I'm taking it Dan never talked to you about this plan.

DEXTER: Why would he talk to me? No, I'm hearing it for the first time. Right now.

CARTER: Even though it was in the paper.

DEXTER: Hey, I make it a point not to read the paper.

(CARTER laughs.)

CARTER: Fair enough. But, look, I'm still trying to piece together the circumstances surrounding his death.

DEXTER: What do you want to know?

(ERNIE *enters rubbing his hands.*)

ERNIE: Sorry I'm late. The new pit boss wants to know why I get a busman's holiday and he doesn't get a break. 'Cause I'm the captain, lard ass. The commander of this corporate bitch. And my card night is sacred. You put in nine years on the same rig, you produce the revenue I pour into this town, you get to dance naked down Wilmington Road. Till then, go suck on a slot machine. Hey, Carter.

CARTER: Ernie, the boat—

ERNIE: It's magnificent, I know. You threw some dice? Had some fun?

CARTER: I lost twenty dollars at roulette.

ERNIE: There's an A T M machine if you want to lose more. (*To* DEXTER.) Where's Ben?

DEXTER: He's not coming.

ERNIE: What?

DEXTER: He's home. With Sally and the kids. His back is out.

ERNIE: So he can't reach into his wallet?

DEXTER: Evidently.

ERNIE: He called you?

DEXTER: He left a message.

ERNIE: Why didn't he call me?

DEXTER: I don't know, Ernie. Maybe he lost your number. Maybe he doesn't like you anymore.

ERNIE: Why wouldn't he like me?

CARTER: Can we get back to that night?

DEXTER: Sure.

ERNIE: Christ!

DEXTER: Dan Harper was a mess when Ben took him inside. I went to the station house for a few hours and happened to be on my way home. I might not have even stopped at his house if I hadn't seen the light on in the attic. I rang the front bell. Ten, fifteen minutes.

CARTER: What time was this?

DEXTER: One A M. So I'm concerned. Because if he's passed out, that's one thing. But what if he's fallen over? Hit his head on the floor? Can't breathe? I went around back. I busted in the door.

CARTER: And you found him upstairs.

DEXTER: Correct.

ERNIE: On a crutch!

DEXTER: Hey, Ernie, the man is in mourning.

ERNIE: I'm in mourning, too, pal. I'm in pain. But I'm willing to share it at the table.

CARTER: So you make the call to the station.

DEXTER: An apparent suicide with a firearm discharged. We brought in the full team. Like I told you.

CARTER: And they dust down the house.

DEXTER: The attic.

CARTER: Not the entire house?

DEXTER: Well, some. Bits and pieces. It was plain to see what had taken place.

CARTER: What did they say about his time of death?

DEXTER: Between eleven and midnight.

CARTER: I'm surprised no one reported hearing the shots.

DEXTER: No one else lives around there.

CARTER: So what about this gun?

DEXTER: What about it?

CARTER: What was the make?

(DEXTER *sighs.*)

DEXTER: A Browning. Semi-automatic. Nine millimeter.

CARTER: I assume his prints were on it.

DEXTER: Of course, they were. And there was powder residue. All over his left hand.

CARTER: Not his right?

DEXTER: He was left-handed, Bartosek.

CARTER: Okay, I forgot about that, I admit, but I'm still trying to understand. I never knew Dan to own a firearm. To even carry an owner's I D.

DEXTER: He didn't.

CARTER: What?

DEXTER: There was no F O I D card.

CARTER: So he got it illegally.

DEXTER: He wouldn't be the first.

CARTER: What about the serial number?

DEXTER: It's been erased. Rubbed out. And we can't raise it.

CARTER: Have you asked the County for help?

DEXTER: No.

CARTER: The State?

DEXTER: The Chief and I decided to keep this thing in-house.

CARTER: I see.

DEXTER: Are we done?

CARTER: Sure. *(Pause)* I assume there's an ongoing investigation.

DEXTER: Into what?

CARTER: Are you serious?

DEXTER: Am I smiling?

CARTER: Well, to start with, how the hell did an ex-congressman illegally get hold of a handgun that led to his death? How did he come to possess all of this child pornography? And how did these pills—?

(DEXTER stands up.)

DEXTER: Look, Bartosek, when you called I thought you had something interesting to add to the case.

CARTER: The reason—

DEXTER: Something my personnel might actually have missed.

CARTER: What I'm saying—

(DEXTER shouts at CARTER.)

DEXTER: Is crap! *(Silence)* The men and women who came out that night and worked their asses off through the weekend in round-the-clock shifts are the best. Your pal had a problem with underage skirt and substance abuse. And because of that he tried to take his own life. No, he did. He succeeded. And for that I'm sorry. But sorrier still is the arrogant prick who thinks he knows everything—

CARTER: I don't know anything!

DEXTER: And cannot live with the facts!

(DEXTER storms off. A moment. CARTER looks at ERNIE.)

ERNIE: He's got no outlets. That's Dexter's main problem. Too much time alone makes a person moody.

CARTER: Did the investigators ever talk to you, Ernie?

ERNIE: Of course.

CARTER: What did they want to know?

ERNIE: Whether or not Dan was sober when I got to the party.

CARTER: Was he?

ERNIE: Who knows? Eventually he became an embarrassment. Ben took him inside.

CARTER: How much longer did this party go on?

ERNIE: An hour. Maybe less. By nine-thirty it was me and Ben. He went back in to check on the host while I picked up a little. And I met him around front.

CARTER: So you locked up?

ERNIE: Ben did. He said the place was secure. Listen Carter, it's not that I mind going over this stuff, but—

CARTER: I know, it's irksome of me to ask, but here's the thing, Ernie. Dan had some plans he was putting together. On affordable housing in the downtown district.

ERNIE: Okay.

CARTER: Is this news to you?

ERNIE: No. No, I remember hearing about it. Reading about it.

CARTER: Did he ever talk to you about this?

ERNIE: A housing development? For the lesser developed? Now that is a conversation I would recall.

CARTER: I take it you don't care for the idea.

ERNIE: Hey, welfare's dead, my friend. Now we all have to earn our way. Or hadn't you heard?

CARTER: And if he had come to you as the manager of one of the most successful businesses in the area—

ERNIE: Excuse me, *the* most successful. I don't mean to blow my own. But that's a fact.

CARTER: What would you have said?

ERNIE: If Dan Harper had told me this was on his political plate, I would have said bust it with a hammer and break it into a hundred pieces.

CARTER: Because it could affect your livelihood.

ERNIE: It could kill my livelihood! I don't mind minorities coming out here to play. If they have money. I have some decent black folks. Some Orientals. But if they're looking to spend their last food stamp, that's no good. I mean, I'm all for celebrating our cultural diversity, but first you have to be able to pay for a ticket to the party.

CARTER: I see.

ERNIE: And we'd have to take in their surroundings on our little cruise. That lot they were talking about is directly downstream. They'd be out on display. It's like Dexter says. The people that are attracted to affordable housing are the same people attracted to nose powder, pistol whippings and prostitution. Look at Grantham. Or, worse, Floral Park.

(Pause)

CARTER: Dexter said this?

ERNIE: Yeah.

CARTER: When?

ERNIE: A while ago.

CARTER: Because he told me he'd never heard of the idea.

ERNIE: Oh. *(He shrugs.)* Maybe he was speaking in the larger sense. Maybe I misconstrued.

CARTER: Maybe. *(Pause)* Thanks for the spin, Ernie.

ERNIE: Anytime, my friend. Come back when you're feeling lucky. Or when you're not.

(CARTER *walks off. A moment. Then* DEXTER *comes back on from the opposite direction.*)

ERNIE: I thought you fell overboard.

DEXTER: What did you say to him?

ERNIE: What did I say? I said his eyes were the color of night. I said the stars pale in comparison to his bright rays.

(DEXTER *suddenly grabs hold of* ERNIE's *hair and pulls his head straight back.*)

ERNIE: Ow!

(DEXTER *leans in and whispers in* ERNIE's *ear.*)

DEXTER: Let's go to the mill.

Scene 6

(ROY's *farm Wednesday afternoon. We hear the sound of a single gunshot, which rips across the acreage. Then* ROY *comes running on, out of breath, carrying his shotgun. He is dressed in casual outdoor clothes.* CARTER *follows with his camera hanging around his neck.*)

ROY: I'm afraid we won't get a second shot.

CARTER: That was close.

ROY: Oh, yes. See that red oak over there? The one with the ripped bark?

CARTER: Yeah.

ROY: He was standing right in front of it.

CARTER: So he's gone.

ROY: But he'll be back tomorrow. Eating my radishes. Gnashing on my tomatoes.

CARTER: I'm surprised that deer hunting is legal in these parts.

ROY: Recently passed. People were outraged, of course. The animal being such a permanent part of the community. But for those of us with farm property the problem is an epidemic. The herd has simply got to be culled.

CARTER: Well, it can't have been an easy decision.

ROY: Oh, it wasn't. I struggled with it myself. But the more these creatures run amok the less chance there is for my trillium.

CARTER: Biodiversity.

ROY: Exactly.

CARTER: And then there's the sheer sport of it.

(ROY *laughs.*)

ROY: Well, I have to admit it's easier than making the trek up to Wisconsin. I'm getting older, Carter. The expeditions are few and far between.

CARTER: Sure. I understand. Even as a kid, I remember Beth talking about her father's hunting trips. His firearms collection. His shotgun.

ROY: Well, the collection's still there, but I'm afraid I don't have the energy to keep it going.

CARTER: At least you've still got the farm.

ROY: What's left of it.

CARTER: How do you mean?

ROY: I've had to sell almost two hundred acres. Incredibly difficult. Seeing how long it's been in the family. Seven generations, Carter. My people came here when the Pottawatomies were still around. Traded bread and tobacco. Built the first dam. The first freight depot. My great-great grandfather fired up the

streets of this town with electricity. We were one of
the first in the nation. The city of light. That's what he
called this place. And so it is. Even today.

CARTER: Well, the high tech people who have taken
over the perimeters would certainly sign onto that.

ROY: Yes, isn't it wonderful? Prosperity. After such a
spotted period. *(Pause)* So what were we talking about?
Before the deer?

CARTER: Dan Harper. He had some plans for that
condemned lot near the center of town. He was looking
into an affordable housing tract.

ROY: That was in the paper. It was a rumor. I
remember.

CARTER: Did he ever mention this to you?

ROY: No.

CARTER: Not even once? In passing? To see how the
idea sounded out loud?

ROY: I can't say that he did.

CARTER: I'm surprised.

ROY: Why?

CARTER: Well, the word on the street is Ernie
Noodleman's riverboat would never have set sail
without your blessing. The tax revenue from that
casino allowed the town to redefine itself. Everyone
attributes the rebirth of Central Avenue to your
persistence.

ROY: It's true. I made a strong case. Got the merchants
organized.

CARTER: Yeah, but that lot is practically sitting on the
church.

ROY: It's three blocks down the road. Maybe four.
What does that matter?

CARTER: And then there's your record of working with lower-income families all across the state.

ROY: Oh, Carter, I don't do that anymore. I'm too old. And the town needs me. My *own* people need me. That's apparent.

CARTER: So if Dan had come to you with this notion—

ROY: He didn't.

CARTER: How would you have responded?

ROY: I would have reminded him that man's chief source of unhappiness on this planet is worry. And worry about worry. God doesn't want us to fret. He wants us to be free of concerns. To stretch out our arms and fully embrace the rich sweetness of life.

CARTER: What does that mean?

ROY: It means that we subscribe to the words of our Lord and savior. "The poor you will have with you. Always." *(Pause)* That property you're talking about is under some dispute. It could be turned into any number of things. Things which, in the long run, given the social parameters of this particular municipality, might have a greater chance of…success.

CARTER: Such as?

ROY: Oh, I don't know. I honestly haven't given the matter much thought. But maybe, possibly… *(He shrugs.)* A park.

CARTER: A park?

ROY: For the children.

CARTER: Right. *(Pause)* Well, I appreciate your time.

ROY: Of course.

CARTER: It's great to see the farm again. It's gorgeous out here, Reverend. Really glorious.

ROY: It is that.

CARTER: Who did you have to sell it to?

ROY: I'm sorry?

CARTER: The two hundred acres? *(Pause)*

ROY: Motorola.

CARTER: So you turned a profit.

ROY: Well, I won't be spending my retirement counting pennies at the poor house.

CARTER: And you still have, what? A hundred? A hundred and twenty acres?

ROY: One forty-five.

CARTER: You could buy the poor house and go condo. *(Pause) If* the prosperity continues.

ROY: Well, I—

CARTER: Do you mind if I impose upon you for one more second?

ROY: No.

CARTER: This handgun.

ROY: Yes?

CARTER: Which Dan evidently used to kill himself.

ROY: I'm listening.

CARTER: Well, he didn't have an I D for it. So he got it illegally. Okay, maybe in D C. But maybe here. Now how would he make that happen?

ROY: I have no idea.

(ROY hears something. He turns sharply. He raises his finger to his lips to indicate silence. Then he sees what he is looking for. He points to a deer off in the distance. CARTER sees it. ROY kneels. He aims his shotgun. CARTER lifts his camera. He takes a step or two back. He snaps a photo of the animal. And as he does we hear the sound of the camera rewinding.

It is rather loud. ROY *lowers his gun. The deer has obviously been scared off by this noise. He turns to* CARTER.)

CARTER: I am so sorry.

ROY: It's alright, Carter. *(He smiles.)* I'll get him next time. *(He wanders off across the farm.)*

Scene 7

(BETH's *kitchen. Wednesday night.* BEN *and* SALLY *are sitting at the table with four mostly empty plates of pasta, three mostly empty glasses of red wine, and two completely empty bottles.* BETH *stands at a distance uncorking a third.* CARTER *is moving around the room and talking at full speed.)*

CARTER: The newspaper's no help. The campaign staff is useless. And the police investigation reeks of amateur hour.

SALLY: Really?

CARTER: Defillipis practically threw a fist at me for asking the most basic questions about his procedure.

SALLY: That seems odd.

CARTER: Yes. Extremely odd. Considering the fact that he's never dealt with anything like this before.

SALLY: What else?

CARTER: Well, Ernie Noodleman is more concerned with his weekly poker game than a local suicide, but he still found time to contradict himself.

SALLY: What did he say?

CARTER: First that Dexter had offered an opinion of the housing situation. Then that he hadn't. Both men claim Dan never talked to them about his plan. Which I accept. But the Reverend?

(BETH *looks at* CARTER.)

CARTER: I'm sorry, Beth. I spoke to him. I did. Because it seemed like Danny would have done the same thing. Even though—

BETH: The divorce.

BEN: Carter—

CARTER: Alright, maybe that explains the lack of communication. Dan wasn't talking to you either. But this thing with the gun—

BEN: Hey, Carter—

CARTER: I asked the Reverend point blank how Dan could have gotten it illegally. He said he didn't know. Had no idea.

BETH: Dad's a stickler for regulations.

CARTER: I'm sure that he is. Believe me, I'm not doubting that. But he goes to the shows, right? He talks to the people who are putting these pieces out on the table. Wouldn't you think that somewhere along the line in thirty years of pursuing this hobby—

BETH: Thirty-one.

BEN: Can I interrupt?

CARTER: He would have met some freak on the political fringes willing to sell anything to anybody?

SALLY: You're saying Roy McAlister associates with criminals?

CARTER: I'm saying he would certainly know how to circumvent the law. Unless he's been wearing his clerical robes over his head. So why lie about it?

(BEN *shouts at him.*)

BEN: Hey!

CARTER: What?

BEN: You're monopolizing the conversation.

CARTER: I am?

BEN: And you're making a hell of a mess out of hearsay.

SALLY: Ben, calm down.

BEN: No. What he's talking about are the drunken ramblings of a sick woman. Beth, here, is gracious enough to invite us all over for dinner and instead of asking about her well-being or yours or mine, he launches into this maniacal tirade against the entire community.

CARTER: Gee, Ben, I'm sorry. How are you?

SALLY: Fellas—

BETH: I just wanted to do something nice before you left town.

CARTER: I'm not going anywhere.

BEN: Fine. Stay as long as you like. But stick to some civility.

CARTER: What is that supposed to mean?

SALLY: This really isn't the place.

CARTER: Why did you take Dan up to that attic?

BEN: What?

CARTER: On the night of his death when he was so wasted. Why not let him sleep it off on the couch in the living room? Or the comfort of his own bed?

BEN: Because that's where he wanted to go. He wanted to sit in his study. To try to collect himself.

CARTER: Unsuccessfully.

BEN: He was asleep in his chair when I left.

CARTER: At nine-thirty.

BEN: Thereabouts.

CARTER: And then he woke up two hours later and shot three bullets into the wall, one of which passed through his head.

SALLY: We should go.

BEN: According to the police report.

CARTER: And what do you think?

BEN: What do I think? *(He laughs.)* I think we don't know anything about anybody. Case in point. You.

CARTER: Me?

BEN: You come here from a place where death and dying is an everyday occurrence. Where you earn your monthly nut pursuing other people's misery. Other people's pain.

CARTER: This from a lawyer?

BEN: But not every situation calls for public scrutiny.

CARTER: Meaning?

BEN: There is no story here!

CARTER: That's fascinating because nine times out of ten when someone tells me that they're sitting on the story.

BEN: You think I know something I'm not saying?

CARTER: I think you're unwilling to explore the possibility that Dan was set up.

BEN: Murdered? Because he wanted to be mayor? Doesn't that seem like attacking the ant colony with a tire iron?

CARTER: Did he ever talk to you?

BEN: We talked all the time.

CARTER: About the housing development?

BEN: No.

CARTER: And if he had?

BEN: I'm not going to get into this with you.

CARTER: Because here you are, in the middle of the real estate mix, and he's contemplating something that could change the economic make-up—

BEN: Carter, I can swear to you on a stack of law books, Dan Harper never came to me with this notion!

CARTER: Okay. *(Pause)* I believe you.

BEN: Oh, well, thank you so much, your investigative holiness. You know what your problem is, pal? The problem you have always had?

CARTER: I'm aching to find out.

BEN: You think you're better than this place. Like the Midwestern sensibility is some sort of a rash you can rub off with global disinfectant. Well, go ahead. Get your hands dirty. Bury yourself in the great unwashed. Then bring home the stink to show the rest of us what we're missing. But here's the truth. This town is part of you. This town *is* you. And no amount of sneering or snide remarks to the people I care about is going to change that. It's a fact of your character. Beth, I'm sorry about this.

BETH: It's alright.

BEN: I have to go. Sally?

SALLY: What?

BEN: I'm leaving.

(A moment. SALLY stares at BEN as if she hasn't been listening.)

SALLY: I'll see you at home.

(BEN looks at SALLY. Then he walks out of the room. A moment. She looks at BETH. She looks at CARTER.)

SALLY: I don't think either of you can understand. But I've lived here...my whole life. I've been with him... *(She nods towards the door.)* Only. Goodness is not something you contemplate. Goodness is action. And I have tried...God, I have tried so hard...to lead a decent—

(SALLY stops. Then she stands up and walks out of the room. CARTER looks at BETH.)

CARTER: What was that about?

(BETH shrugs. Then she refills his glass. She sits at the table.)

CARTER: You're not drinking.

BETH: No.

(Pause)

CARTER: So what do you think?

BETH: About what?

CARTER: What he said? Am I doing this to make a point? When the point doesn't exist?

BETH: Possibly.

(Pause)

CARTER: And Danny?

BETH: What?

CARTER: Was he capable of taking his own life?

BETH: He was capable of anything. But I didn't know the man anymore. So I can't say. *(Pause)* What do *you* think?

CARTER: Regarding?

BETH: Ben's comment.

(CARTER laughs.)

CARTER: I think he's full of it. He doesn't know the first thing about what I do. Why I put myself through it. Seeing men and women who I've talked to, had a meal with, turned into pieces of meat. Or the remains of my colleagues scraped off the side of a mosque. Attempting to walk away from *that*. To put *that* into words. For no recognition. No money. Security. Family. A wife. *(Suddenly the wine glass shatters in his hand.)* God.

BETH: Are you okay?

CARTER: Yes.

BETH: Let me get a towel.

CARTER: I'm alright.

(BETH grabs a napkin, kneels down in front of CARTER, and takes the glass out of his hand.)

CARTER: Sorry.

BETH: I'm cutting you off.

(CARTER laughs.)

CARTER: Okay, so maybe he's onto something, the son of a bitch.

BETH: How so?

CARTER: Oh, Beth, we don't want to get into this.

BETH: What?

CARTER: Look, I see it now, okay? I understand. All I ever wanted to do was to make an impression on the people I love. On you. Mostly on you. I knew you were Danny's girl, but it didn't matter. I still wanted you. Still wanted to be with you. Even after we all went away to college. Even after you were married, Beth. You know this. Why do I need to say it?

BETH: Don't say anything if it makes you unhappy.

CARTER: And when things went bad between the two of you, when you found out I was in Manhattan, and came to see me, and we had those six days—

BETH: Five.

CARTER: It was six, Beth. I counted. I remember.

(BETH *finishes cleaning* CARTER's *hand. She stands up. He wraps the towel around his fist.*)

CARTER: I thought maybe there was a chance. I knew it was ridiculous. That it was wrong. But I couldn't help myself. Lying there naked with you on that mattress in Hell's Kitchen. The heat. That summer heat. The smell of your body. The scent of your breath. Finally. For a moment I was…whole.

BETH: I liked it, too.

CARTER: And when you left that afternoon, sneaking off while I was in the shower, and that note— *(He reaches into his wallet and pulls out a crumpled up piece of paper.)*

BETH: Oh, Carter.

(CARTER *reads.*)

CARTER: "I can't do this anymore." I've had a lot of time to think about that sentence. The meaning of it. Seven and a half years. Almost eight. Attempting to make sense out of five words. What is "this?" What is "anymore?" Who "did" what to whom?

(CARTER *puts the paper down on the table.* BETH *walks around behind him. She wraps her arms around his shoulders.*)

BETH: I had to go back to him.

CARTER: I know.

BETH: To give it another try.

CARTER: I understand.

BETH: That doesn't mean it was nothing.

CARTER: What was it?

(BETH *shakes her head.*)

BETH: I was lost in D C. Hated that place. The pace. The insincerity. And Dan treating me like an accessory. I was supposed to support him. Endorse him. Offer the shell, but show nothing of myself. And I was sick to death of it. I had to get away. For a day. A week. To be with somehow who— *(Pause)* I kept thinking back to school. How I thought my life would make perfect sense if only I could be with this guy. How everybody loved him. Especially me. I couldn't stop watching him. The way you couldn't stop watching me.

CARTER: I wasn't aware I was that obvious.

BETH: Oh, I liked it, Carter. But I couldn't help myself. I was—

CARTER: Stuck.

(BETH *nods.*)

BETH: And when it started to come apart, I found myself thinking about you. The one I should have turned to. The one I should have been watching.

(BETH *runs her face against* CARTER's *hair. His hands go up to reach for her. She slides down on to his lap. They kiss. He grabs onto to her. She pulls away for a moment. She looks at him.*)

BETH: There's no one else here.

CARTER: Where's Zoe?

BETH: Spending the night at Shannon Kent's.

CARTER: I thought they were on the outs.

BETH: They made up. *(She kisses him again.)* Stay with me?

CARTER: I can't.

BETH: Stay?

CARTER: Beth— *(He pulls away.)* I can't do this anymore.

*(*BETH *and* CARTER *stare at each other. Suspended in space. Silence)*

END OF ACT ONE

ACT TWO

Scene 1

(BETH's bedroom. Thursday morning. BETH lies on top of CARTER who has a bandage on his hand as a stream of sunlight fills the room.)

CARTER: Well… *(Pause)* So much for the strength of my resolve.

BETH: Are you sorry?

CARTER: No.

BETH: Seriously?

CARTER: No, I am seriously not sorry.

(Pause)

BETH: Did you get any sleep?

CARTER: A little. I woke up around four-thirty completely disoriented. At first I thought I was back in Beirut. Then Ben's. Then I felt you curled up around me. For a moment I thought I was still asleep. Still dreaming. *(Pause)* How about you?

BETH: I had the best sleep I can remember. *(Pause)* I like having you here.

CARTER: It's strange. For me. Being with you again.

BETH: Why?

CARTER: Oh, I don't know. In one way it feels like a century has passed since the last time we were together. In another it feels like it was last week.

(BETH *kisses* CARTER.)

CARTER: You look beautiful.

BETH: I know I don't.

CARTER: No, you do. There's something about you. First thing in the morning. Here. I want to do this. (*He reaches into the bag beside the bed and pulls out his camera.*)

BETH: No. (*She pulls the sheet up around her.*)

CARTER: Let me take your picture.

BETH: Absolutely not.

CARTER: One shot.

BETH: Carter—

CARTER: Please.

(BETH *sighs. She pushes her hair back.* CARTER *takes a photo.*)

CARTER: Thank you.

BETH: That's for personal use only.

CARTER: Believe me, I'd never publish it. Well, maybe. But I'd split the proceeds.

(BETH *laughs and slaps* CARTER.)

BETH: When did you starting taking photographs?

CARTER: When did I start? A while back. Two, three years.

BETH: But why?

CARTER: You don't want to know.

BETH: Carter—

CARTER: You don't.

(A moment. BETH *looks at* CARTER. *He sighs.)*

CARTER: I was in a situation. There was a story I was working on about these refugees in a neutral site, a safe zone, supposedly. Well, they all got taken out. Murdered. Men, women, and children. By mercenaries with our weapons. Our guns and our grenade launchers. It was a whole expose I was going to write about American arms. Who gets them. What they do with them.

BETH: And?

CARTER: The story never got published because I didn't have the necessary proof. The correct documentation of the crimes. Now I take pictures. Of everything. So the next time I stumble onto truth, it'll be—

BETH: Irrefutable.

CARTER: Yeah. *(He laughs.)* Nice pillow talk, huh?

BETH: It's alright. I like the way you are with me. Always have. I don't feel like you're trying to change my mind about anything. To alter my...what?

CARTER: Politics?

*(*BETH *laughs.)*

BETH: Oh, Carter, I don't know that I have any.

CARTER: You must.

BETH: I don't. I don't believe in them. Maybe I did at some point, but Washington washed them right out me.

CARTER: Yeah, I can understand that.

BETH: I went through this rotten period after Zoe was born.

CARTER: With Dan?

BETH: With everybody. I was ailing from all the fundraisers and fat contributors. These callous men. Touching me. Like they owned me. I started drinking. Too much. Experimenting with some…illicit substances.

CARTER: Coke?

BETH: How'd you know?

CARTER: Hey, it's all over that town.

BETH: Well, I fell right into it. Spiraled. Down and out. It's why I don't use alcohol now. Don't even take aspirin. Anyway, Dan found me one night in a less than sober state. He filed. And the teeth came out.

CARTER: What did he do?

BETH: Oh, *he* didn't do anything. He had his legal boys come after me. Full force. They tried to wreck me. Ruin whatever was left of my name. I fought back. I won. Got my girl. Got out of that arena. But ever since. Politics. It's like a dirty word someone stuffed in my mouth.

CARTER: So what do you believe in now?

(BETH *shakes her head.*)

BETH: A quiet house. A warm bed. *(Pause)* This.

(BETH *kisses* CARTER *again and pulls him down onto the bed.* ZOE *walks into the room with an overnight bag. She stares at them.*)

ZOE: Are you having a sleepover?

(BETH *and* CARTER *break off the kiss and sit up.* BETH *pulls the sheet up even tighter. He makes certain that he is covered with a blanket.*)

BETH: Oh, uh…hi, honey.

ZOE: Hi.

BETH: How was the party?

ZOE: Fine. Shannon ate most of the stuffed pizza. And Alice Beisterfeldt bit her on the foot.

BETH: Don't you have school today?

ZOE: We're off.

BETH: Oh.

ZOE: Can I watch a movie?

BETH: Sure, I…let me get that set up for you.

(BETH *walks out of the room with the sheet wrapped around her leaving* ZOE *staring at* CARTER *and the camera on the edge of the bed.*)

ZOE: Are you taking naked pictures of my mother?

CARTER: No. No, I was…showing her how it works. The camera.

ZOE: Can you show me?

CARTER: Okay.

(CARTER *hands* ZOE *the camera and indicates how to look through it.*)

CARTER: You look through here. Focus here. And when the frame is filled—

(ZOE *snaps a picture of* CARTER *in bed.*)

CARTER: Yeah, that's…how it works.

ZOE: Cool.

CARTER: Can I have that back, Zoe?

(ZOE *hands it to* CARTER.)

CARTER: Thank you. *(Pause)* Listen—

ZOE: I like to draw, but the drawing never comes out the way I want.

CARTER: Well, that takes…practice.

ZOE: That's what Mom says. She says I'm in too much of a hurry to get everything right. But I want to get it right. What's the point if it's not right? So I draw all the time.

CARTER: That's wonderful.

ZOE: I made a painting of the nature preserve. With the path. And the wild flowers. I did a whole bunch. A series.

CARTER: Wow.

ZOE: They didn't really look like anything.

CARTER: Still, I'd love to see them.

ZOE: I gave them to Dad. He liked them. I went over there one Saturday and let myself in.

CARTER: You let yourself in?

ZOE: He kept a key in the birdhouse. It was our secret. We wrestled and then we made French toast and then we hung them up. The paintings. Not the toast.

CARTER: Oh.

ZOE: He told me he'd decided something he wanted me to know.

CARTER: What was that?

ZOE: He was going to stay here. In this town. In his home. And I could come over anytime I wanted. Anytime Mom would let me. *(Pause)* Why do people do that?

CARTER: Do what?

ZOE: Why do people have kids if they're going to live in different houses?

CARTER: I— *(Pause)* It's complicated.

ZOE: That means you don't want to tell me.

CARTER: No, I...men and women. We come together for the strangest reasons. We rarely know what we're doing. We have this idea of how it should be. How we want it to be. Perfect. We want it to be perfect. But— *(Pause)* Why did Alice bite Shannon on the foot?

ZOE: What?

CARTER: Did Alice know she was going to bite her friend when she went over to her house?

ZOE: No.

CARTER: Adults do the same thing. We think we have it all figured out. Like we know who we are and exactly how we're going to be. But we don't. We can never tell when we're going to hurt someone. And children— *(Pause)* They're like our highest aspiration. Our ideal. Do you know what that is?

ZOE: Sort of.

CARTER: They are us in our best sense. But we lose track of that. We get angry with ourselves. With each other. And your mom and dad, they wanted to be together. Believe me, they tried. And they couldn't. But this much I know. Separate houses. Different cities. It doesn't matter. They loved you. They both still love you. A lot.

ZOE: A lot?

CARTER: To the far side of the sun and straight on to forever.

(ZOE laughs.)

ZOE: I like that. *(Pause)* What are you doing here?

CARTER: Me? I'm, uh…

(BETH comes back into the room wearing a robe.)

CARTER: Saved.

BETH: It's Sally.

CARTER: What?

BETH: On the phone. *(Pause)* She's calling from the hospital.

Scene 2

(A hallway in the local hospital. Thursday noon. Immediately following. LOIS is in a hospital gown and sitting in a wheelchair. SALLY is in her nurse's uniform and stands beside her. She is attempting to reconnect an intravenous tube into LOIS's arm.)

LOIS: I don't like needles.

SALLY: I don't like patients pulling out their I V.

LOIS: I'm not your patient.

SALLY: You are as long as you're in this hospital.

LOIS: I didn't ask to be brought to this—

(SALLY sticks the needle into LOIS's vein.)

LOIS: Ow!

SALLY: If you'd hold still it wouldn't hurt.

LOIS: If you'd let me walk out that door I'd be happy to hold still. At home. On the couch.

SALLY: We'll get you home. As soon as we can. But first we're going to finish running these tests.

(CARTER comes into the room.)

CARTER: What happened?

SALLY: She—

LOIS: I can speak for myself.

CARTER: What?

SALLY: She collapsed.

LOIS: Thank you. That is not actually what occurred. I was feeling poorly.

SALLY: The postal carrier found her face down in her garden.

LOIS: I took a tumble.

CARTER: Mrs G—

SALLY: Her blood alcohol level was off the charts.

LOIS: I'd been celebrating.

CARTER: Oh, yeah? What? Exactly?

LOIS: It's Thursday. I like Thursdays. I always have.

CARTER: Oh, Christ.

SALLY: You're lucky you didn't go up in a blue flame.

LOIS: Is that your professional opinion or personal hyperbole?

SALLY: You need help.

LOIS: With what?

SALLY: Your drinking.

LOIS: I would say I'm doing pretty well all by myself.

CARTER: Mrs G, if you want to kill yourself, there are easier ways.

LOIS: Goddamn it to hell, Carter, I am not trying to kill myself!

CARTER: Then what are you doing?

LOIS: Grappling.

CARTER: With?

LOIS: My failing health.

CARTER: Then do something about it. Get some treatment. See a doctor.

LOIS: I don't like doctors. And I prefer to treat myself.

CARTER: Yeah, to a bottle and a half a day.

LOIS: Two. If you have to know. Get your facts straight.

CARTER: Do you think there's some sort of moral superiority in being the town drunk?

LOIS: What a thing to say!

CARTER: Do you?

LOIS: Listen to me, Mister Bartosek, when you've battled it out to my age, when you've raged against the great ignorance, you can rail me with insults, but not a minute before.

CARTER: What exactly are you talking about?

LOIS: Do you know what I was doing in my garden? *(Pause)* Do you?

CARTER: Looking for mint?

LOIS: Planting. And replanting. And tending to the soil. Because the perennials are a constant. No matter how bad the weather, how blistering the winter, they still occur. And reoccur. They never disappoint. They always inspire. *(Pause)* When I started teaching I thought I could do the same with children. Root out the mess around their murky heads. Encourage them to look straight on into the sky.

CARTER: And we've all disappointed you.

LOIS: Not all.

CARTER: But you gave us the tools. The essential skills. And we should have used them better.

LOIS: I should have taught you better.

CARTER: You were a first-rate teacher.

LOIS: Not what to think.

CARTER: You were.

LOIS: Or even how.

CARTER: Listen to me—

LOIS: But why. Why it's important to study a book.
A single book. Any book. Not knowledge for its own
sake. Spit on that. Useless as refuse. But knowledge
for betterment. Strong and abiding betterment. For our
streets. Our cities.

CARTER: Our collective souls?

LOIS: Possibly.

CARTER: Yeah, well, I hate to tell you, Lois, but that
wasn't your job.

LOIS: It should have been. *(Pause)* Have you been
asking around?

CARTER: About Dan?

(LOIS nods.)

CARTER: Yeah.

LOIS: And?

CARTER: Nowhere. It goes…nowhere. Maybe he talked
to someone about his politics. Maybe he made an
enemy or two. But I don't know who that is.

LOIS: No.

CARTER: And the town—

LOIS: Yes?

CARTER: It's nothing like what I remember.

LOIS: What do you remember?

CARTER: Well, it wasn't much to look at, I admit.
Certainly not as pretty as it is today. Not as purified.
But there was an openness. Real openness. One family
moved in, everyone was there to say hello. Another
moved out, and we were sad to see them go. We talked
about them. How much they'd meant. What they'd
contributed. This kid was lost in the woods once. Two
days. Tommy—

SALLY: Hawbecker.

CARTER: Right. We all went looking. Hundreds of people. Found him sleeping by the stream. Took him home. Another time the hospital put out a call. Evelyn O'Brien, eighty and almost blind, needed blood. The donors lined up around the block. Bill Egan got his hand caught in that power mower. Couldn't work. No insurance. Money arrived anonymously. Everybody contributed. People who had nothing offered something. *(Pause)* I don't what it was, but we had it. That thing we're supposed to aspire to. A sense of purpose. Of pulling together for someone other than... oneself.

LOIS: Well, it's not that anymore.

CARTER: No. *(Pause)* I think I should leave things alone.

LOIS: Maybe so. *(Pause)* Carter?

CARTER: Yeah?

LOIS: I need to sleep now.

CARTER: Okay.

(SALLY comes toward LOIS.)

LOIS: How about some rubbing alcohol with a straw?

SALLY: I—

LOIS: Oh, Sally, please, buy yourself a sense of humor.

(SALLY wheels LOIS off. A moment. Then she returns.)

CARTER: So besides the obvious—

SALLY: Yeah?

CARTER: What's wrong with her?

SALLY: Well, we're still waiting on the results of these tests and Doctor Wyman won't be in till after—

CARTER: Oh, come on, Sally.

(SALLY sighs.)

SALLY: The heart. She's got a cardiac disease. There's only so much we can do.

CARTER: Of course.

(Pause)

SALLY: So is that what we are?

CARTER: What?

SALLY: Bad flowers? Weeds that went wrong?

CARTER: I don't know. *(Pause)* I have to get out of here. *(He starts to go.)*

SALLY: Listen—

(CARTER turns and looks back at SALLY.)

SALLY: I should have said something sooner.

CARTER: About what?

SALLY: Ben told you that Dan never came to him about the housing development. Which is true. Which is accurate.

CARTER: But?

SALLY: Ben went to *him*. *(Pause)* He took Dan out to dinner at Gillespie's. Just the two of them. Guys' night out. I called from the house. On the cell phone. Ben forgot to hang up. And I heard it. *(Pause)* I heard the whole thing.

CARTER: Tell me.

SALLY: Ben had gotten wind of Dan's idea. Someone had talked to him about the development. And he tried to talk Dan out of it. Ben said it would be bad for the community. For the kids. Danny got angry with him. He swore at him. Cursed him for being so closed minded. Then he left. *(Pause)* Ben came home. I asked how dinner was. He said fine.

CARTER: Did you talk to anybody else about this?

SALLY: No. There was no reason to. I thought it was nothing.

CARTER: Bad news, Sal.

SALLY: What?

CARTER: I don't think it's nothing. *(He walks out of the room.)*

Scene 3

(The conference room in BEN's law firm. Thursday afternoon. Immediately following. BEN comes into the room followed by CARTER.)

BEN: Remember how we talked about civility? Remember that, Carter? That doesn't include confronting me while I'm attempting to close a deal.

CARTER: Why didn't you tell me?

BEN: Because I didn't think it was any of your business.

CARTER: Not my—?

BEN: Look, certain things were said.

CARTER: What?

BEN: That's what I'm about to tell you.

CARTER: So what's stopping you?

BEN: Sit down.

(CARTER doesn't move.)

BEN: Sit. Down.

(A moment. Then CARTER takes a chair. He stares at BEN.)

BEN: Now. I have an office full of malcontents on the other side of that wall. This conference room is private, but not *that* private. Keep. Your tone. Civil. *(Pause)* I get the impression you think this has somehow all been easy for me.

CARTER: I don't have any thoughts on the subject, Ben. Easy or not. I don't know what to think.

BEN: I did talk to Danny.

CARTER: About the development.

BEN: Yes.

CARTER: You were against it.

BEN: Of course, I'm against it. It's a lame ass idea. A simple solution to a complex problem.

CARTER: The problem being—?

BEN: I don't have the problem. Dan had the problem. He brought it with him.

CARTER: Which was?

BEN: The notion that he could somehow apply his utopian concepts of how a society should function to a town he hadn't been connected to since he was eighteen. Concepts that hadn't cleared the table in Washington. Leftovers from some ideologue's bad lunch.

CARTER: You thought it was impractical.

BEN: At the least.

CARTER: Impossible.

BEN: In another world, it might work. Not where I live.

CARTER: To want to do something honorable with a piece of land that—

BEN: Honorable? *(He laughs.)* Do you have any idea what I do everyday? What I have done everyday since we threw our graduation caps up into the air? I build. Something. A home. A family. A business that is barely hanging on due to the huge overhead of working in one of the fastest growing municipalities in the state. If the market shifts here, I go down. And I take Sally and the kids with me. So I swim. In these waters. In the place I have worked to make better by being an active part of it.

CARTER: I thought you were doing well.

BEN: I am doing well, Carter, but in order to maintain, to simply have enough loose change left over at the end of the month to pay the pizza man, I have to do even better. That's the crux of the equation. To get out of debt, I have to accumulate more.

CARTER: Why?

BEN: To expand. To keep pace. Otherwise, I die.

CARTER: And Dan's plan—?

BEN: Would have wrecked the real estate scene. Pure and simple. People around here would have panicked. They'd have sold their property overnight. My business would go bust. My two lots would be worthless. And I'm back to filling out tax returns for H & R Block.

CARTER: So after you talked to Dan, after he disagreed with your fatalistic take on the situation, you went home, put together some materials, and pushed them through the mail slot at the newspaper. *(Pause)* Come on, Ben, you can tell me. The thing reeks of you. Unable to convince an old friend he's wrong, unwilling to take no for an answer, you act surreptitiously. Silently. When the town is still asleep. A story in print. Some fireworks. And no one'll know who lit the match.

(Pause)

BEN: It's not as simple as that.

CARTER: Yes or no?

BEN: I had to do something.

CARTER: Yes or no, Ben?

BEN: Yes!

CARTER: Okay. *(Pause)* And when the spark sputters, when Dan simply laughs it off saying he hasn't made up his mind on this or any other topic, you kill him.

BEN: That is so goddamn wrong I can't even begin to explain.

CARTER: Tell me where I'm wrong, Ben.

BEN: There's more going on than you're aware of.

CARTER: Like what?

BEN: Than *I'm* aware of.

CARTER: Who first told you that Dan was thinking about doing something with that condemned lot?

BEN: I— *(Pause)* He did.

CARTER: Sally said that you got the information from someone else.

BEN: She's lying.

CARTER: Why?

BEN: To protect me.

CARTER: From who? Yourself? Is the crime any less because two people are involved instead of one? *(Pause)* How's your back?

BEN: What?

CARTER: Your back that was bothering you. The feeble excuse you came up with to get out of the card game. Is it any better?

BEN: What are you—?

CARTER: Dan had painkillers in his system. Percocet. A name you couldn't even pronounce three days ago.

BEN: So?

CARTER: It's a narcotic that's good for any number of things. Including stress. Of the lower back.

BEN: I don't take—

CARTER: Not now, you don't, but I stopped by Lowell's Pharmacy this morning. I said I was there to pick up your meds. George Lowell said he hasn't filled a prescription for you since last spring. I asked if he'd ever given you Percocet 'cause I'd heard it worked wonders. He gave me the nod. *(Pause)* You were bartending for Dan that night. Lois Garrity told me so. It would have been the easiest thing in the world to slip ten or twenty of those babies into his beer.

BEN: I swear to you that I did not kill Dan Harper.

CARTER: You already swore to me. On a stack of law books. It could have been Bibles with Christ's signature, Ben. I don't believe you. I think you're covering something up.

BEN: You don't want to go any further with this.

(CARTER throws the chair across the room at BEN and screams.)

CARTER: Don't tell me what I want to do! *(Pause)* Is that civil enough for you?

(Silence. BEN backs off. CARTER starts to go.)

BEN: Where are you going?

CARTER: To find the rest of the club. *(He walks out.)*

Scene 4

(The Old Grist Mill. Thursday night. DEXTER and ERNIE sit drinking beer and tequila. A collection of empty bottles and shot glasses line the table. They have been here for a few hours. We hear the sound of acoustic rock and roll as CARTER enters the bar and goes to them.)

DEXTER: Bartosek—

ERNIE: Hey, have a drink. Sit down. We're doing a few shots.

DEXTER: Ernie had one hell of a night.

ERNIE: Got these first-class losers lined up for some district managers meeting. Morons with money to puke. They come to my ship. We turn a little wheel. *(He pulls a wad of bills out of his coat pocket.)* Biggest take the boat has ever seen.

CARTER: Congratulations.

ERNIE: This is tip money. What I will use tomorrow morning to wipe my ass. Want some?

CARTER: Uh, no.

(ERNIE shouts at him.)

ERNIE: We are footloose, Carter! We are fancy free! We are having a hooray-for-me-and-fuck-you kind of life!

CARTER: Yeah, I can see that.

ERNIE: What do you want? Tequila? Beer?

CARTER: Nothing.

ERNIE: Hey, I'm buying.

DEXTER: Which happens once a millennium. Believe me. Take advantage.

CARTER: I'm not thirsty.

ERNIE: So what are you doing here?

CARTER: Looking for you. I checked at the ship and the station house. Both of your homes. Then I remembered. The Old Grist Mill.

ERNIE: They fixed it up nice, didn't they? Bar lights. Saloon decor. This could be the start of a historic district. But you know what I say? *(He leans forward and whispers.)* Burn all the history. *(He laughs and raises his shot glass.)* Cheers.

DEXTER: Yeah.

(*They both drink. A moment.* CARTER *doesn't move.*)

DEXTER: So what's up?

CARTER: Talk me through it again.

ERNIE: Through what?

CARTER: Danny's suicide.

ERNIE: Hey, we've done this. Twice already.

CARTER: Everyone leaves. The party's over. You stay to clean up.

ERNIE: Like the sunny Samaritan I am.

CARTER: Then you go around to the front of the house.

ERNIE: That's right.

CARTER: To wait for Ben.

ERNIE: Yes.

CARTER: And keep watch.

ERNIE: What?

CARTER: In case anyone comes back. You're there. Standing in the driveway. Surrounded by all those woods. You can warn him. Ring the bell. Bang on the door.

ERNIE: And I'm doing this why?

CARTER: Because Ben is upstairs planting the pornography.

ERNIE: Okay.

CARTER: Which you supplied.

ERNIE: Me?

CARTER: That's right. Of course, you could be inside helping him with the details, but it makes more sense to divide responsibilities. Be the alarm. The lookout. Because the clock is ticking.

(A moment. Then DEXTER *stands up.)*

DEXTER: I got to go pee.

ERNIE: Where would I get pictures like that?

DEXTER: Hey, Ernie, there's no reason to—

CARTER: A contact from the boat. A transaction under the table. Who knows? Child porn costs money. And you keep telling me how much you have. Of course, maybe it wasn't you. Maybe it was a cop with access to contraband.

*(*DEXTER *turns and looks at* CARTER. *Then he approaches him. Nose to nose.)*

DEXTER: Sorry?

CARTER: You might have picked up the photos at the same time you got the gun. The weapon with no serial number. Which can't be traced.

*(*DEXTER *stares at* CARTER.*)*

DEXTER: Do you have any idea how difficult it would be for me to get a hold of a Browning M 1903? Even if I wanted to? The cops don't carry them. And the punks can't afford them. They're almost impossible to locate.

CARTER: Then you expect me to believe that Ben set Danny up all by himself. Without your help. *(To* ERNIE*)* Or yours. *(Back to* DEXTER*)* That he doped him up. That he helped him upstairs while Ernie here stood around shuffling his feet. That he fired two shots into the wall and a third through Dan's head.

DEXTER: You think Ben Oglesby killed your buddy?

CARTER: Unless it was you. *(To* ERNIE*)* Or you.

ERNIE: Whose shoe did you scrape this idea off of?

DEXTER: Let me get this straight. You're calling us, the three of us, killers. Murderers.

CARTER: What would you do to protect this place, Dexter? To keep it free of undesirables? To insure that you had the easiest possible ride from Commander to the next highest position? Would you knowingly lie on a police report? Plant false evidence?

DEXTER: Get out of here before I lose it, Bartosek.

CARTER: Would you pull a trigger?

DEXTER: Get out of my face.

CARTER: I'm asking you!

(CARTER *grabs* DEXTER's *arm and* DEXTER *lashes out. He throws a series of fast punches at* CARTER *who lands on the floor.* DEXTER *kicks him in the gut. Once. Twice.* ERNIE *recoils into the corner of the room. He winces.*)

ERNIE: Hey, Dexter—

DEXTER: Son of a bitch thinks he knows everything!

(DEXTER *kicks* CARTER *one last time. Then he turns and walks out.* ERNIE *comes over to* CARTER. *He looks at his battered body lying on the floor. He sighs.*)

ERNIE: You should have let me buy you a drink.

Scene 5

(*The office of* ROY *at the First Presbyterian Church. Thursday midnight.* CARTER *sits in the second chair facing the desk and staring up at a single source of light. His face is bleeding from the beating and he still has the bandage on his hand. He is wrapping his elbow in a fresh bandage as* ROY *comes into the room.*)

ROY: Carter.

CARTER: Hello, Reverend.

ROY: My God, you look…what happened?

CARTER: I ran into a cop with the side of my face and most of my stomach.

ROY: Let me get you a fresh cloth.

CARTER: No.

ROY: Some water.

CARTER: I'm alright.

ROY: But the blood—

CARTER: Leave it. *(Pause)* Thanks for coming.

ROY: Well, I was surprised to get your call. This late. And from the office. I assumed Beth was here. Catching up on some correspondence or—

CARTER: No, I let myself in.

ROY: Oh.

CARTER: Did I get you out of bed?

ROY: Not exactly. I was working on a sermon.

CARTER: A sermon.

ROY: For Sunday.

CARTER: Uh-huh. *(Pause)* What's the subject?

ROY: Well, I— *(Pause)* Healing. How to go about healing. As a community. I want to bring a sense of closure to the horrible atrocity of last week. To speak to the congregation in a way that will allow us all to move forward.

CARTER: Not an easy assignment.

ROY: No.

CARTER: Especially for some.

(Pause)

ROY: Was the front door open? I was sure we'd locked up, but sometimes—

CARTER: I broke in. *(He touches his elbow.)*

ROY: You—?

CARTER: I busted a window. Into the storeroom. I found some tools and took out the bolt on the office door.

(ROY *turns and looks back at the way he came.*)

ROY: Why?

CARTER: To get inside. *(Pause)* I'd been driving around for hours. Attempting to make some sense of what I know. What I suspect. Then I found myself outside the church. And I remembered something.

(Pause)

ROY: Carter, you're obviously in a state. I'm sorry for that. But I can't—

CARTER: Shall I tell you what I've been able to ascertain?

ROY: About?

CARTER: Danny's death. His suicide. Real or alleged.

ROY: Alleged?

CARTER: You nod if you think I'm on the right track.

ROY: Look, we have to—

CARTER: Dan wants a housing development. He looks into it. Does some research. Then he comes to you. You can tell me I'm wrong here, but I'd call you a liar in the house of God.

ROY: Carter, he never came to me.

(*A moment. Then* CARTER *reaches for a date book at his side. He opens it.*)

CARTER: "February Twenty-third. Ten A M. Dan Harper."

(ROY *goes to his desk and sees that the drawer has been broken into.*)

CARTER: The lock was simple enough to snap after the window and the door.

ROY: Oh, God, now this is really—

CARTER: Are you in the habit of writing down appointments that don't happen?

(A moment. ROY *sighs. Then he acquiesces.)*

ROY: Alright, he wanted to meet with me, but we didn't talk about this housing plan.

CARTER: I'd almost believe you if it wasn't for the next two entries.

ROY: That book—

CARTER: "February Twenty-fourth. Twelve-thirty. B Oglesby."

ROY: Ben had some personal problems that he wanted to discuss. I—

CARTER: You asked him to speak with Dan. To try to reason with him about his plan.

ROY: No.

CARTER: In fact, you told him to. Or strongly hinted that if he did as you suggested you'd put in a good word. With two other men.

ROY: Who are you—?

CARTER: "February Twenty-sixth. One P M. Rupert Frost and Paul Ehrenhart."

ROY: Both of whom happen to be elders of this church.

CARTER: When they're not working at First Security and Trust. Well, working is too strong a word. As I recall they run the place. Rupert is senior man in charge of loans. And Paulie's president of the bank.

ROY: Meaning?

CARTER: Ben wants to expand his business. But I'm guessing he'd be considered a bad risk. He's behind on his other loans. And there's nothing left to use for collateral. So you tell him that you'll do everything you can to facilitate the deal if he'll agree to work on Dan.

ROY: I would never—

CARTER: Which he does with mixed results. Actually, no results. So he plants a story in the paper. And then another. And when nothing comes of either one, you suggest, strongly suggest, that he go to Plan B.

ROY: Which is?

CARTER: The decimating of Dan Harper's character. *(Pause)* Reluctantly, Ben agrees. He knows it's the only recourse. Danny's plan is no good for anyone except a few gratuitous outsiders. But now he's at a loss. He understands real estate, but not how to ruin a man. So he turns to his cohorts at the card table. And the three men concoct a scheme. Ben has the painkillers. Ernie has the porn. And Dexter'll be back at the house at one A M to find Dan in his doped up state. Dead asleep. With the pills running through his system and the pictures all over the floor. *(Pause)* Only it's not enough. *(Pause)* Danny could bounce back. He could take the offensive and turn the affair to his advantage. After all, this is America. Everyone deserves a second chance. And he's still got two weeks to the election. So when Ben reports back to you and says this is what it is, this is what we're going to do, you say, no, *this* is what you're going to do.

ROY: I—

CARTER: Set him up.

ROY: Carter.

CARTER: And kill him.

ROY: Where did you—?

CARTER: The weapon, Reverend! A Browning M 1903! That's why I'm here. The cops don't carry them and the criminals can't afford them. They're almost impossible to locate. In short, they are collector's items. *(Pause)* I may have a fact or two turned around here, but I think the basic premise is correct.

(ROY doesn't move. Then he slowly goes to a window. He looks out.)

CARTER: Please don't talk to me about the social parameters of this particular municipality.

ROY: You have no perspective—

(CARTER screams at ROY.)

CARTER: On what? Cold-blooded murder? Blowing out a man's brains?

(ROY turns on CARTER and shouts.)

ROY: One hundred and sixty-five years! *(Pause)* That's what I have invested in this town. Heading back through seven families. My people have endeavored to make this a better place. Livable. And, yes, profitable. Because without some recompense all our good works are fodder for the bonfire. Black smoke. So I have carried on that tradition in the hopes of turning our economic disadvantage to advantage. Single-handedly. I cleaned up most of this strip. We got the word out. The place was reborn. And business is once again flourishing. Our women wear good clothes. Our children are cared for. The Metra people finally want to build a train station out here connecting us to their suburban line and that big city on the lake. But do you know what? We don't need them. Because we're self-sufficient! *(Pause)* My ex-son-in-law wanted to alter that. He thought that the influx of all this new money had changed us. It hasn't changed us. It allows us to be what we are. Only more so. It liberates us. He didn't understand that. He wanted to spread it around. To strangers. Outsiders. People who have no idea what it means to construct something out of nothing. Out of wilderness. A river. Trees. And open space.

CARTER: So you killed him.

(ROY *shakes his head.*)

ROY: If even the smallest percentage of what you say is true, Carter, and that is a highly-unlikely if, with nothing to back it up, no real proof, no confession, then I can tell you this. And listen. There was never any plot to take a man's life.

CARTER: But you did it anyway.

ROY: I left that party at nine-fifteen with Beth and Zoe. I drove them home. I slept in her guest room.

CARTER: So you could have an alibi.

ROY: I was tired.

CARTER: Then Ben.

ROY: With his wife and children.

CARTER: Ernie.

ROY: The same.

CARTER: What about Dexter?

ROY: At the police station. His superior saw him. And Ben and Ernie's neighbors saw them. Believe me, I've checked. None of them was near that house when Dan died. No one knows what happened! (*He drops down into his chair behind the desk.*) No one knows what happened.

CARTER: *If* it were true.

(*Pause*)

ROY: We would have done what was necessary to make it seem like he was addicted to narcotics and that he was dangerous. We would have put that pistol in his hand and fired two shots into the wall. That is all.

CARTER: And the third shot?

ROY: I have gone over and over and over it in my mind. I've talked to Ben. The others. The house was sealed. No one else knew. No one else suspected. *(Pause)* I can only come to one conclusion.

CARTER: What's that?

ROY: Drugged...drained of all energy and coherent thought...he suddenly wakes up...sees the object in his hand...stares into the barrel...his fingers twitch...his knuckle locks—

CARTER: No.

ROY: The thing goes off.

CARTER: Impossible.

ROY: It is the only explanation! *(Pause)* And for those of us responsible...for those of us who laid the foundation for this tragic circumstance...we would have to live with this...horrendous bloodshed...this... sin...for the rest of our lives.

CARTER: Maybe longer.

(Pause)

ROY: Yes, maybe longer.

(The church bell starts to toll midnight. CARTER stands looking down on ROY. He pockets the date book and walks out of the office.)

Scene 6

(The attic of Dan Harper's house. Friday morning. Five A M. CARTER *sits behind the desk, his head slumped forward, asleep. A moment. Then* BETH *appears in the doorway. She sees him and calls out to him.)*

BETH: Carter?

*(*CARTER *doesn't move.)*

BETH: Hey, Carter?

*(*CARTER *sits up and takes in his surroundings, the room, the dried blood on the walls, the bullet holes,* BETH.*)*

CARTER: What are you doing here?

*(*BETH *comes into the room.)*

BETH: I couldn't sleep. I thought you were…I thought you'd be coming back to my house. So I called over to Ben's and he said you hadn't shown up there. Said you and he had a fight in the afternoon.

CARTER: Yeah, we had a little disagreement.

BETH: I went out driving. Looking for you. I saw the car parked out in front. The door was open. I—

CARTER: What time is it?

BETH: Five A M.

CARTER: Where's Zoe?

BETH: With a neighbor. *(Pause)* How's Mrs G?

CARTER: Dying. If she doesn't start to take care of herself. Find something to do besides soaking up alcohol.

BETH: I'm sorry. I…I know how much she means to you.

CARTER: Yeah, well… *(Pause)* It's her decision to make. *(He goes to the window and looks out.)* It's almost morning. I got to figure out what I'm going to do.

BETH: About what?

CARTER: Some information that's come into my hands.

BETH: What?

CARTER: I think it's better if we don't talk about it, Beth. Till I know what I'm doing. Where I'm going with this.

BETH: Is it about Dan?

(A moment. Then CARTER *nods. He comes to* BETH. *He kneels down. He looks her in the eyes.)*

BETH: What happened to your face?

CARTER: Listen to me. I'm aching here. I don't know what to do.

BETH: Someone hurt you?

CARTER: No. I mean, yes, but…what's happening…I have to do something. To go forward with this. And people…certain people…are going to get whacked. People we like. We care about. *(Pause)* Family.

BETH: Who?

*(*CARTER *shakes his head and turns away. He stands, goes to the desk, looks down.)*

CARTER: I'm driving around last night, two, three A M, the only car out on the road, and I see this twenty-four-hour photo lab at one of the strip malls. They developed my film while I sat in the parking lot and listened to Christian radio. It's all there, Beth. The documentation of a week spent kicking through the ashes of my childhood. *(He laughs.)* The faces I used to know. *(Pause)* I thought maybe if I could come up here to this attic and sit and look at those faces coolly, objectively, I'd figure out what to do. *(He sorts through the photos, one at a time.)* A naked man sitting in the bedroom of the woman he loves. He's a little embarrassed. Her daughter is taking the picture. Then there's the woman herself. With a sheet covering her fine lines. And a half smile on her lips. Then a minister, a man of God, pointing a shotgun at some stupid animal he's about to slaughter. A police commander with a tight fist wrapped around his little town. A casino manager who's sweating insecurities. Their friend who's buried in the bad debts of a life that's spinning out of control. His wife who blinds herself to their situation by staying in perpetual motion. This room. *(He stops. He stares at the picture. Then he turns and looks at the wall.)* Why didn't I see that before?

BETH: What?

CARTER: Why didn't I see? *(Pause)* He couldn't have pulled the trigger.

BETH: What?

CARTER: Not the third shot. Not the one at his head. Look. *(He goes back behind the desk, sits down, and pantomimes holding a gun.)* Okay, he's here. He's asleep in this chair. Face forward on this desk. Knocked out with the gun in his hand. Suddenly he sits bolt upright. He's completely disoriented. What happened? What am I doing here? I'm holding something. What is it? A semi-automatic. Why? He turns it toward him. *(He holds his one hand in the other.)* He's staring directly into the barrel.

BETH: Carter, please, I—

CARTER: Bang. It goes off. Accidentally. He goes backwards. The gun falls onto the floor.

BETH: Why go through this again?

CARTER: Because he was high on painkillers. Muscle relaxers. And the gun powder was only on one hand. His left. The right was clean. *(Pause)* Unless he was holding the gun with both hands, steadying the one with the other, there's no possibility that there could have been a clean shot through the center of his head into the wall directly behind him. *(Pause)* Somebody else had to be holding that gun for the third bullet. Not Ben. He's home in bed. To all reports. So's Ernie. Dexter's at the station. Somebody else was here. Someone who let themselves into the house.

BETH: You got in.

CARTER: That's because Zoe told me about the key in the bird house.

(CARTER holds it up. He looks at BETH. She shifts uneasily.)

CARTER: Like she would have told you.

BETH: Why would she tell me?

CARTER: I'm a strange man sitting in her mother's bedroom with a blanket wrapped around me. She talks. That's what seven-year-olds do. She must have said something. *(Pause)* She did.

BETH: Yes, okay, she mentioned it. In passing. It was supposed to be their secret, but—

CARTER: Then why deny it?

BETH: I'm not denying anything.

CARTER: Oh, God, Beth, don't, don't tell me, please don't—

BETH: What?

CARTER: Last Friday. A week ago. You left the party with Zoe. With your dad. He took you home. He spent the night. In the spare room.

BETH: Of course.

CARTER: And you stayed there. You stayed in that house.

(A moment)

BETH: I—

CARTER: You were here.

BETH: No.

CARTER: There's blood on the walls. Enough to make me sick when I first saw it and you haven't even flinched. You'd seen it before.

BETH: Why would I—?

CARTER: Give me your hands.

BETH: What?

CARTER: Your hands. The residue of gun powder can stay on the skin for weeks. Months. Even with cleaning. And scraping. There are still particles. They won't come out. *(Pause)* Please.

(Slowly, reluctantly, BETH places her hands in CARTER's. He turns them over. He stares down. He closes his eyes. He clenches her fingers.)

CARTER: Tell me what happened.

(A moment)

BETH: The problem with old churches is that sound carries. The acoustics are impeccable. It's nice for the minister, for the choir, but not so practical if you're trying to have a meeting behind closed doors. *(Pause)* I knew that Dad had been talking to Ben. That they had differences. With Dan. What he was planning. And they had a plan of their own. And then we were all at that party. And I saw Dad slip Ben a cigar box. The sort of box he always kept his pistols in. Then Dan started acting strange and we all went home. I put Zoe to bed. I left her there with Dad asleep. And I came back here. I saw Ernie out front. Pulling this sealed package out of the trunk of his car. Ben came down and took it from him. Then I heard two shots. I figured… *(Pause)* I thought that they'd killed him. That it was over. Ben came back out. And the two of them left. I waited for a few minutes. I came inside. And I found him. There. Passed out at the desk. With a gun in his

hand. And two shots in the wall. And these pictures—
(Pause) I knew what they were doing. What they were
attempting to do. But they hadn't done it right.

CARTER: Beth—

BETH: He tried to ruin me, Carter. At my lowest ebb.
He left me. And he filed. With no concern for my
situation. No responsibility for my state. He took
me into a court of law and told everyone in that city
that his wife was a dope fiend not fit to care for his
daughter. *His* daughter? *(She laughs.)* He hadn't even
done the math to figure out that— *(She stops.)*

CARTER: What?

(BETH shakes her head.)

CARTER: She wasn't his?

BETH: No.

CARTER: Then who?

(BETH looks at CARTER. A moment. He takes it in.)

CARTER: Oh, my God. *(Pause)* Oh, Christ.

BETH: I didn't know how to tell you.

CARTER: She's mine?

BETH: She's ours, Carter! And he wanted her! He was
willing to take my life apart, incident by incident, after
all that I had done for him. Everything I ever was.
What I aspired to. Tossed into his brilliant career. But
that doesn't count. Not in that town. So I had to fight
back. I had to become the selfish bitch he accused me of
being. I got my girl. I got out. I came here. *(Pause)* Then
one day he shows up and it all starts again. He finds
it. My one refuge in the world. The only place I feel
safe. He wants to be near his daughter. Who knows?
Maybe he's going to set the legal apparatus on me.
One more time. Take her away. Forever. He says that's
not the reason. He claims that he wants to be of use.

Of service. A man of the people. *(She cries out.)* Who
are these people? What have they ever done for us?
For me? *(She is starting to fall apart.)* And, no, it doesn't
matter that seeing him on the street everyday, sitting in
the same church, the same pew, is like a punch in the
gut, a kick in the head. What matters is the big picture.
Well, I am so sick of the big picture and his face smack
in the middle of it that I could— *(Pause)* The gun was
right there. It's like they set it up for me. Like they
wanted me to do what they didn't have the courage to
complete. I lean him back in the chair. I take hold of his
hand. *(Silence)* Oh, God. Oh, my God. *(The full weight of
what she has done is finally beginning to catch up with her.)*
I can't believe I did this.

CARTER: Oh, Beth.

BETH: Can't believe I… What have I…?

*(BETH collapses into tears. CARTER grabs onto her. He holds
her.)*

CARTER: You didn't know what you were doing.

BETH: I knew *exactly* what I was doing. I wanted that
bastard. Dead.

CARTER: Christ.

BETH: Don't let go.

CARTER: I won't, I won't, I promise, I'll hold on.

BETH: Don't go.

CARTER: Calm down.

BETH: What are we going to do?

CARTER: We're going to make a call.

BETH: No.

CARTER: We have to, Beth. Go to the cops. The
authorities.

BETH: Why?

CARTER: Why? *(He laughs.)* What do I have to explain?

BETH: No, no, look, listen, please!

CARTER: Beth—

BETH: Everyone thinks it was a suicide.

CARTER: So?

BETH: Let them think that. Let them blame themselves. I'm the only one who knows what actually took place in this room.

CARTER: And now me.

BETH: And now you.

CARTER: No, see, I've got no choice here.

BETH: They'll take her away.

CARTER: Zoe? Maybe. I don't know, but—

BETH: We can't let them do that.

CARTER: *We* are not in this together.

BETH: But we could be! *(Pause)* We could have a life here, Carter. The one we could have had all this time. If we'd been smart. We could wake up every morning. Like today.

(CARTER looks at BETH.)

CARTER: I can't even begin to let myself think about this.

BETH: Help me.

CARTER: I can't.

BETH: Help her.

CARTER: Beth—

BETH: I know what I did. I do. It's unspeakable. But punishing me, putting me in a hole, will not do her any good. She deserves better. *(Pause)* Carter.

CARTER: I wish that I could.

BETH: But you can.

(CARTER *disengages himself from* BETH, *gets his bag, and goes. She runs to the door. She screams after him.*)

BETH: You can!

Scene 7

(*McAlister Park. The following September. Saturday morning. We hear the sound of birds chirping. Children laughing.* SALLY *stands looking out across the area. A moment. Then* BEN *approaches her from behind.*)

BEN: Look at them run.

SALLY: Oh, yeah. Round and round and round they go. Battering into each other.

BEN: Benji didn't want to come.

SALLY: I know.

BEN: Now he's having the time of his life throwing himself down those slides.

SALLY: Why did they have to make them so big?

BEN: I don't know. Because they could. Check out that sandbox.

SALLY: God, it's huge. Enormous. I'm afraid Joey's going to bury all the toddlers.

BEN: Hey, I'm just happy to see him in long pants.

SALLY: Well. (*Pause*) Well, they've obviously done a first-class job out here. With the architecture. The materials.

BEN: Yes, they have.

SALLY: And the kids deserve it. They do. A place to call their own.

BEN: Absolutely.

SALLY: Before life catches up.

BEN: Hey. *(He grabs her from behind and gives her a kiss on the back of the head.)* Don't be morbid.

SALLY: I'm not being morbid. I'm...reflecting.

BEN: Well, don't be reflecting.

(ERNIE and DEXTER come on with beers and cigars.)

ERNIE: Hey, hey, no petting in the park. That's the rule. I'm putting up a sign.

BEN: Hey, guys.

DEXTER: How's it going, Oglesby?

SALLY: Where are the twins?

ERNIE: Scarfing down the free eats.

DEXTER: What little is left after Dad here sucked down half the spread.

ERNIE: So allow me to offer my congrats.

BEN: About what?

ERNIE: The firm. The expansion. I hear business at the legal palace is booming.

BEN: We're doing alright.

ERNIE: Better than alright is what my sources say. Everybody's knocking on your door. And you know what?

BEN: What's that?

ERNIE: You deserve it.

BEN: Thanks.

ERNIE: I mean, I know I got a bonus coming that's more than most people retire on, but I can still take pleasure in my friend's small achievements, right?

BEN: Well, we're not the only ones coming up in the world.

SALLY: What do you mean?

BEN: Tell her, Dexter.

DEXTER: Hey, it's not official.

BEN: The Chief's stepping down and the Commander here is two steps away from his office.

ERNIE: He's already redecorating.

SALLY: They want you to be Chief?

DEXTER: That's the rumor.

ERNIE: So now we all get to see what it's like to live in a police state.

(They laugh as ROY *comes on.)*

ROY: Does anybody need anything?

BEN: No.

ROY: We still have chicken-kabobs. And shrimp. Sally?

SALLY: I'm okay.

ERNIE: Hey, there he is. The man of the hour.

DEXTER: It's spectacular, Reverend.

ROY: Impressive, no?

DEXTER: Definitely. A state of the art playlot. With how many swings?

ROY: Twenty-six. Plus a field house, a miniature golf course, three baseball diamonds, a sled run, and an indoor skating rink.

DEXTER: Congratulations.

ROY: Well, I certainly didn't do it all myself.

ERNIE: No, but without you spearheading the effort, the lot would still be empty. An eyesore. Useless.

BEN: I was glad to hear about the dedication.

SALLY: Me, too.

ERNIE: McAlister Park. It's definitely the right moniker.

ROY: Well, it's as much for her as for me. For our children. And their children.

ERNIE: Speaking of which.

(BETH *and* ZOE *come on.* ZOE *has a camera around her neck. She runs up to* ROY *and he swings her through the air.*)

ZOE: Grandpa, look what I got! From Mexico! It focuses and everything!

ROY: A camera.

ZOE: Can I take your picture?

ROY: Of course.

BETH: Dad, the ceremony's about to begin.

ROY: Yes, I know, sweetheart. Welcome home. You look wonderful.

BETH: Thanks.

SALLY: You got some sun.

BETH: A little. Hello, Ben. How is everybody?

BEN: We're good, Beth.

ERNIE: I think that's an understatement.

BETH: Yes, I know what you mean. We were driving up and I was thinking how fresh everything looks. How fall is right around the corner, but the town still feels like it's swimming in some eternal summer.

ERNIE: We're having a Labor Day Soiree out on the boat.

DEXTER: Oh, lock it up for a minute, would you?

ERNIE: Hey, I'm just letting people know. As a courtesy. Or is that against the law?

(CARTER *comes on.*)

CARTER: There's almost no place to park on the street.

BEN: No.

CARTER: It's like the entire town has turned out.

SALLY: I think they have.

CARTER: The entire county.

BEN: How was Cozumel?

(BETH *and* CARTER *start to speak simultaneously.*)

CARTER: Oh, it was alright, we—

BETH: Wonderful, I—

(Pause)

CARTER: Go ahead.

BETH: Well, the three of us had the nicest time.

ZOE: Carter taught me how to snorkel! And took me sailing!

BETH: I'm so glad we went. It was good to get away for a few weeks.

SALLY: Every couple should have a honeymoon.

BEN: Even the ones who don't tell anyone when they're getting married.

CARTER: Well, that was my idea. My...preference. I wanted a small affair. With Zoe. And the Reverend.

(ROY *corrects him.*)

ROY: Dad.

ERNIE: Did you get the glassware?

CARTER: We did. Thanks, Ernie. But we really didn't need any presents.

ERNIE: Hey, everybody needs presents.

ZOE: Look what I got!

DEXTER: How's the new post?

CARTER: Fine. *The Dispatch* needed a new editor. And I needed the position. We'll see how much we like each other. But I'm hoping it'll stick.

ROY: Carter, while you were gone, something…

CARTER: What?

ROY: Maybe this isn't the right time.

BETH: What is it, Dad?

ROY: Lois Garrity, she…

(Pause)

BETH: Oh, no.

ROY: She passed on. *(Pause)* I was there. Ben was there, too. It was fast. Painless, I think. She simply…slipped away.

(Pause)

CARTER: I should have been there.

ROY: No.

CARTER: I should have—

ROY: I think it's better that you weren't.

SALLY: She was delirious, Carter. Didn't know who any of us were. What we were doing there.

ROY: Anyway. *(Pause)* We're starting up a fund. In her name. In her memory.

CARTER: Well, that's…thoughtful.

ROY: For scholarships. For the best and the brightest. To send them out in the world.

BEN: I think Mrs G would be pleased.

CARTER: Yeah, I…tend to agree. Though I don't know. I can't speak for her. I know she believed in it. Learning. The importance of… *(He is starting to lose it.)* Finding that part of yourself which is…connected to the whole. Acting on it. Everyday. In a way which is…

(BETH *goes to* CARTER.)

BETH: Don't.

CARTER: Which allows for the possibility…at least the possibility—

BETH: Don't blame yourself.

CARTER: What is that called? What is the word for… wanting to do something? To make a difference? A critical difference? And being absolutely frustrated in that effort? Not through circumstance? Or the callousness of others? But yourself? You can't kick-start yourself? You know what you should do? What's correct? And can't? Because of your…inability? Your…

BETH: Carter—

CARTER: Lack?

(*Silence. The circle of friends and family stands awkwardly for a moment. Then* BEN *speaks.*)

BEN: Well, I think we all want to make a difference.

ROY: We do, Ben.

BEN: We try.

ROY: Yes.

BEN: But there are things we can do for others and then there are things that we have to do for…

(ZOE *walks a few steps back and aims her camera at* ROY *and the others.*)

BEN: Ourselves. (*Pause*) I suppose.

ROY: Well, maybe we should be—

(ZOE *takes a candid picture of them.*)

ROY: Hey, that wasn't fair. Nobody was ready. Okay, if we're going to do this, let's do it right.

(He gathers them together for a photo.)

ROY: Everybody in here. Come on, Beth. Ernie, Dexter, let's go.

SALLY: Please don't take my picture.

ROY: Come on, Sally, you, too. Ben. Carter?

CARTER: Right.

(They all move together. They attempt to smile for the camera. ZOE takes another shot.)

ZOE: I got it!

(A marching band in the distance starts beating out a tune.)

ROY: Okay, let's go. Let's get this ceremony over with. Then we can eat again!

(ROY leads BEN, SALLY, ERNIE and DEXTER off across the park. BETH goes to ZOE. CARTER stands in place.)

BETH: Let's be careful not to use all the film.

ZOE: Why?

BETH: Well, we might want to take some photographs when we get home. *(She turns and looks at CARTER.)* Carter?

(CARTER is staring at ZOE.)

CARTER: Come here.

(CARTER kneels down and reaches out. ZOE rushes into his arms. He holds her. Tight. He is shaking.)

CARTER: To the far side of the sun and straight on to forever.

(ZOE laughs. He releases her. And she runs off after ROY. BETH approaches CARTER. She touches his chest.)

CARTER: I don't know if I can do this.

BETH: You have to try.

CARTER: I don't know if I can.

BETH: We need you.

CARTER: I know, but—

BETH: *She* needs you.

CARTER: But what does she really need, Beth? A father who loves her? Takes care of her? Is there for her? Or a father who does the right thing?

BETH: There are a hundred right things that cross our path everyday. And this is one of them. And she loves you. *(She kisses him.)* I love you. *(Pause)* Let's go to the party.

(Then BETH *takes* CARTER *by the hand and leads him off after the others into the pure light of this perfect day as the band gets louder and louder.)*

END OF PLAY

.

www.ingramcontent.com/pod-product-compliance
Lightning Source LLC
Chambersburg PA
CBHW052119090426
42741CB00009B/1875